CHOSEN
GENERATION

6 principles and short stories equipping students to grow in self-awareness and become transformational leaders.

ROBERT B. VANN

Robert B. Vann
Robert Vann LLC
5515 Brickell Rd
Norfolk, VA 23502
www.Robertbvann.com
info.robertbvann.com

Printed in the United States of America
First Printing 2022
First Edition 2022

ISBN 978-1-5136-9589-1

10 9 8 7 6 5 4 3 2 1

To my future children!

TABLE OF CONTENTS

INTRODUCTION

Imagine yourself standing in front of a 12-foot giant. He has enormous arms with rigidly defined muscles and a wingspan of about 10 feet. His legs stand like trunks of oak trees, broad and defined, with feet that sit heavy on the ground like 100-pound weights hosting seven toes on each foot. His chest is broad, his stomach is toned, his neck is thick, and his head is raised, complimented by a golden face shield riddled with battle scars. His voice, as deep as a lion's roar, rages miles around while his eyes pierce the soul of any man, and his hands aggressively grasp a battered shield of bronze forged by fire and a sword of terror 6 ft long. As you stand 20 yards in front of him with only a few soldiers behind you, and he stands across from you with a mighty army chanting his name, you may wonder, "How did I get here?" You didn't wake up this morning thinking that you would be the one standing toe to toe with a mighty giant, but somehow you did! What about the other soldiers with you or even the ruler of your kingdom? How did you end up being the one having to fight this giant? Another question, why does this always happen to you! You're always the one!

As you stand 20 yards in front of the giant, he seems to be unimpressed with your presentation. You're only 5' 8", with bronze-colored skin pierced by the sun. Your arms are lean, bruised from previous battles, legs worn but stable due to constant training, and feet covered with shin-high boots. Chest protected by a chest plate of armor. And a face that shines bright as the noon-day sun. Your dark black hair shines in the sun and blows through the light breeze, and your eyes sparkle as their brown tint focuses on the giant without flinching, showing that you are not afraid. Your lips are soft yet firm, and your cheeks round. Your hands yield a sword passed down from your father, and your shield is at its last, but you're ready. You've fought many battles, won and lost, but this one is different. Your heart races in your chest and beats like a drum on Sunday morning, your forehead is gleaming with sweat, but within, you believe you will win. "Kill him!" the opposing Army screams to the giant, "Kill Him!"

With your feet firmly planted in the ground, the vibrations of their war cry pulsing up through your feet and spine, you decide to charge forward. Your brown eyes locked in on the giant as he is belting a loud roar. Each step towards him feels like a step towards death, but you won't stop. Step after step, you raise your sword, and the giant digs his feet into the ground as he braces for impact. He shakes his head in disbelief as he believes he will defeat you like the others, but the giant doesn't realize what type of Chosen warrior you are. You take one last deep breath as you leap off the ground like a gazelle, pouncing towards the giant, slashing your sword ferociously towards him. By the time he tries to adjust his body to prevent himself from being harmed by your sword. It cuts smooth through his body as fast as lightning, and the giant falls in defeat.

Dramatic, probably for some, but for me, this story paints a picture of our everyday lives. See, the giant in this story represents the challenges, hurdles, and opposition we face daily. For you, that may look like: having trouble with reading comprehension, breaking down math equations, passing the ASVAB exam, getting accepted by your college of choice, or your peers, committing to your relationships, discovering who you are, identifying your passions, establishing your interests, or even graduating from school. Other giants could be dealing with separated/divorced parents, a drug-addicted sibling, confused sexuality, warring with depression, contemplating suicide, possessing a degree with no employment, thousands of dollars of student loan debts, attending courses but unable to afford college books, or being a first-generation college student. All of these are giants!

After reading this story, we can learn a few things from this warrior. We can see that he was: courageous, willing to fight for what he believed in, confident about his abilities, wasn't easily intimidated, trained to be a great warrior, and a remarkable leader, but ultimately, he believed in himself. Now, why is this important? This point is important because though he was a skilled warrior, trained to fight, had weapons of warfare, and won previous battles, he wouldn't have been able to win the fight if he didn't believe in himself. If he didn't believe in himself, he wouldn't have stepped up to fight. If he didn't believe in himself, he wouldn't have been able to fight alone. Ultimately, if he didn't believe in himself, he wouldn't have had the courage to lead. Therefore, this warrior's victory was a byproduct of his self-awareness and will be the key to our victory as students, people, and leaders.

Becoming self-aware is not a destination. It's a journey. It's a journey filled with ups, downs, highs, and lows. It's a journey that requires sweat equity, tears, smiles, cries, late nights, early risings, sacrifices, and often setbacks, but amid it all, you will gain the superpower of self-awareness. Yes, self-awareness is a superpower that many people don't have. Look around you; how many of your friends have the superpower of self-awareness? Be honest; you know you have some friends who are putting on for the gram, stunting on Facebook, and flexing on Tic Tok! You know some of your friends are showing out for their boyfriends and girlfriends just to get attention! You know how it is because sometimes you may find yourself faking to be accepted. But I want to give you the courage to take the masks off and put your cape on because self-awareness is the superpower that's going to take you to infinity and beyond!

This book provides six principles to grow self-awareness and position you as a transformational leader. Self-awareness and transformational leadership are connected because you can't be a transformational leader if you're not self-aware. The world needs more self-aware leaders because they lead with purpose. They have a sense of mission and are committed to seeing others around them.

Well, what does this have to do with you! I need you to grasp this concept of self-awareness and transformational leadership because I need you to be the leader in your peer group. I need you to be the leader in your home, class, dorm, job, student lounge, courtyard, food hall, and park. I need you to be the one in the group that sets the tone and pushes others to greatness. I need you to be the one who isn't satisfied with the status quo, mediocrity, poverty, or getting by. I need you to set the standard, and the only way to set the ideal is to be the standard. Transformational leaders lead from the front but can reach back to the back and push them forward.

Therefore, the Six CHOSEN principles introduced in this book will equip you to become more self-aware and give you the tools to become an effective transformational leader. The Six Chosen Pillars are:

1. <u>C</u>ommit to Character

2. <u>H</u>onest about Priorities

3. <u>O</u>pen about Emotions

4. <u>S</u>erious about your Future

5. <u>E</u>arn to Own

6. <u>N</u>ever Settle

These six pillars have transformed my life and given me principles to lean on in times of stress and uncertainty. As a student, 11-year military veteran, Pastor, non-profit exec, mentor, author, and speaker, I've utilized these six pillars to keep me focused and motivated. For example, let's use the giant story as an example. If you were to go to war with that giant, but you weren't serious about your future, you wouldn't have had enough courage to fight for your life. If you had fought him but were willing to settle for defeat, you and your fellow soldiers would've been defeated. If you had battled him, but you weren't committed to Character, you wouldn't have had the grit or belief within yourself to step up to the challenge.

See applying these pillars will help you become an effective leader and successful in every area of your life and become a better you. Think about it this way; when do you think the warrior in the story became successful? Was it after he defeated the giant or before? I say, before, because a warrior isn't determined by their actions; they are determined by their heart. Therefore, as you continue to grow and read this book, know that you are a product of what you think about yourself. Whatever you believe you can do, you will do, but whatever you think you can't do, you won't! Henry Ford said it best by saying, "Whether you think you can or can't, you're right." This statement reveals a dangerous reality.

So why did I write this book?

I wrote this book because, after 15 years of working with youth, students, and young adults of all kinds, I've learned something; Y'all are dope!! I mean, dope!! But a lot of students like you don't even know it. You don't know how special and important you are. You don't know how valuable your voice and opinion are in the lives of your friends. There is someone in your circle who desires your approval. Someone in your family admires your ability to persevere and be resilient. You are dope! I wrote this book because I'm tired of seeing this generation get swallowed up by comparison, depression, doubt, low self-esteem, and suicide. I'm tired of hearing about teen pregnancies, racial discrimination, sexual assaults, violence, and gender discrimination. I'm tired of seeing this generation fall to the perils of cyberbullying or feeling like they're too small, thick, short, tall, fast, slow, ugly, or pretty. I wrote this book to say, "Heyyyyyyyyyy, We are all special and Chosen to do something great." I wrote this book to tell you that you are essential, unique, seen, influential, and needed today more than ever before. I wrote this book to help you identify your core self, identity, mission, vision, and skillset so that you can help and change this world for the better. So I'm telling you and the millions of students alive today around the world you are a CHOSEN GENERATION.

What do I mean by the Chosen Generation? I suggest that you are the generation of students who will change this world for the better and flip it upside down. You are the next Kobe Bryant, LeBron James, Drake, Taylor Swift, and Mark Zuckerberg. You are the next entrepreneurs, athletes, doctors, lawyers, mechanics, biologists, architects, music engineers, artists, philanthropists, teachers, professors, veterinarians, scientists, consultants, speakers, authors, politicians, and others. You will add value to this world, and it will not take you long to do it. The young are chosen because they're strong, but the older are chosen because they're wise. Now is your time to be great and utilize your talents, gifts, values, and resources to make this world better.

<u>What is the Purpose of this Book?</u>

This book aims to equip you with the tools necessary to grow in self-awareness and become a transformational leader. Whether you are a leader right now or maybe one in the future, this book will help you improve your leadership skills or adopt a new set for your roles in the future. So, What are Self-awareness and transformational leadership all about?

- <u>Self-awareness</u>- knowledge and awareness of your Character, emotions, and desires over time

- <u>Transformational Leadership Theory</u>- is a process where leaders and followers raise each other to higher levels of motivation and morality.

Becoming more self-aware is the most important journey we should be focusing on, but while we are on this journey, we should use our trip to transform the lives of others and become transformational leaders. Why transformational leadership, and why do I need to learn about that right now? It's simple, the sooner, the better!

When I was young, I mainly lived for myself, very selfish and single-minded, but it hindered my ability to make a difference. However, this book will give you the tools to become a transformational leader who has a mission to serve others for the greater good and equip them to become self-aware as well. This book will teach you how to use these transformational principles to prepare your younger siblings to be more confident and reliant upon themselves rather than on the likes of others. These transformational principles will help you navigate through relationships and be more selective about your friendships. These transformational leadership principles will help you make better decisions about your education, religious practices, financial stewardship, health & wellness, and romantic relationships. Transformational leadership is a leadership style that promotes the well-being of all and will be the key to your next level of success!

So take a good look at yourself right now? Look at how you act and think about yourself! Look at who you hang around with and what you do in your spare time. Look at how you view education and the possibilities for your future. I also challenge you to assess your current values, commitments, and priorities because all of these things may be different by the end of this book. By the end of this book, your friends may not be the same, your goals may not be the same, and how you think about yourself may not be the same!

So go on the journey with me as you grow in self-awareness, become a transformational leader, and defeat every giant that tries to get in your way. Are you readdyyyyyy? Let's gooooooo!! I'll see you in Chapter 1!

Chapter 1

Influence: The Result of Self-Awareness & foundation of Transformational Leadership!!

Understanding & Mastering your Influence!

"The key to successful leadership is influence, not authority."
— Kenneth Blanchard

It is terrible to be popular and not know it, but it's even worse to know that you are and not use it for good. There are many ways we can influence those around us while at school. Still, our ability to influence others goes far beyond the classroom. Consider popular influencers like Simone Biles, Mahalia, Trae Young, Anne Frank, Drake, Tom Holland, NBA Youngboy, Taylor Swift, Denzel Washington, and even A Boogie Wit da Hoodie. We could also mention others like Treyvon Martin, Breonna Taylor, George Floyd, Martin Luther King Jr., Alexander Grandbell, Madam CJ Walker, Abraham Lincoln, Einstein, George Washington Carver, Langston Hughes, Etta James, and Dr. Eric Thomas. These are names of people who recognized, mastered, and utilized their influence to change the world and did it their own way. It doesn't matter whether you choose to create an app, start a podcast, invent a new hair product, start a business, attain a degree, become a doctor, or pursue an uncommon interest; you can do it your own way and style. I promise other people will appreciate you for it. So let me let you in on a little secret: You have the Power of Influence; Yes YOU! Therefore, in this chapter, we will discuss how to recognize, master, and utilize self-awareness and the power of influence to positively affect the lives of others around you.

FIGHT THE POWER!

During the summer of 1989, American hip hop group, Public Enemy, introduced a song entitled "Fight the Power." The song encouraged citizens of all races and creeds to fight for what was right for everyone, especially concerning the travesties African Americans were facing at the time. They created this mantra to get those who listen riled up and ready to move towards action. Today, I want to challenge you to view this statement differently! I want you to fight against the powers of negativity, doubt, fear, shame, defeat, depression, comparison, anxiety, and loneliness that try to overcome you daily. I want you to fight against the powers of normalcy, generational cycles, lack, poverty, laziness, bitterness, anger, and abuse. I want you to fight these powers today so that you can possess the capability to control your tomorrow.

Let's stop right here and define what power is. Power is defined as the possession of control, authority, or influence over others. This is important to understand because whether you know it or not, you are being controlled or influenced by something from the moment you wake up. Sometimes it is connected to the desire to succeed. What that influence looks like is different for us all. That influence might be pleasing your parents, hanging out with your friends, impressing a cute guy or girl, gaining a scholarship, making the team, fulfilling a childhood dream, obtaining a top-tier paying job, starting a business, getting you and your family out of the neighborhood you're in, or earning a degree; something(s) is influencing you to do what you do. In other words, something is impacting our decision-making, even down to the foods we eat. Therefore, by understanding what influences you, you will gain self-awareness and use your influence to help others transform their lives.

What is Self-awareness, and why is it important to you?

Self-awareness is one of the five competencies of Social & Emotional learning identified by the Collaborative for Academic, Social, and Emotional Learning. The organization CASEL expressed that Self-Awareness is made up of an individual's cognitive, behavioral, and affective competencies. The concept focuses on social, emotional, behavioral, and character skills that support the school, workplace, relationships, and community success. They are often considered "soft skills" or personal attributes rather than explicit targets of instruction. Social & Emotional Learning decrease suspensions & expulsions and helps students engage with each other, their teachers, and their learning positively. These five competencies include:

1. Self-awareness

2. Social-awareness

3. Relationship skills

4. Self-management

5. Responsible Decision making

These competencies provide the framework many educational institutions use to teach, equip, and lead their students to become more well-rounded and productive world citizens. Many teachers, staff, and administrators focus on these five competencies and utilize them to create lesson plans to establish more healthy and productive environments for themselves and their students. After learning this, I decided that these five competencies are excellent and well-needed, but genuinely believe that Self-awareness is the foundation of them all. The Collaborative for Academic, Social, & Emotional Learning organization (CASEL) defines self-awareness this way: Self-awareness- the capacity to reflect on one's own feelings, values, & behaviors.

This definition is key to remember and will be the definition we will use for the rest of this book. So, strap in because it's time to start your journey!!

Social Development

Mr. Erik Erickson, the creator of the Stages of Psychosocial Development theory, reveals 8 stages of social development that he believes every human goes through from birth to death. Each step consists of a particular age group and specific virtue that each person should gain within its stage. For example, stage 5 includes youth between the ages of 12 and 18. Within this stage, Erikson states that youth ages 12-18 have the option to either discover their identity or experience role confusion. He suggests that if one successfully masters this stage, their experience will result from fidelity, the quality or state of being faithful, accuracy in details, or exactness. He believed that mastery of this stage for teens would allow them to enter adulthood with a positive self-awareness and discover their purpose.

During Stage 5, adolescents search for a sense of self and personal identity through an intense exploration of personal values, beliefs, and goals. Children are also becoming more independent and look more toward future careers, relationships, families, housing, and how they'll fit in society. During this stage, youth and young adults have to learn their role as adults. They will constantly reexamine their identity to find out exactly who they are!

In H. L. Bee's book, "The Developing Child," he writes, "what should happen at the end of this stage is 'a reintegrated sense of self of what one wants to do or be, and of one's appropriate sex role'" (1992). Failing to establish a sense of self can result in role confusion or identity crisis! Even a 2019 study of more than 6,500 12-15 year old's in the US found that those who spend more than 3 hours a day using social media might be at heightened risk for mental health problems. For this reason, I wrote the book in hopes of assisting in the healing process concerning mental and emotional wounds that lead to our youth making decisions that could affect their destinies. The hope is that with time there will be a reduction in-school suspensions, childhood pregnancies, suicide attempts, and mental health issues with the right encouragement. Because I have learned that as you grow in self-awareness, you can become stronger and more aware of your passion. It also equips one's life to become an influence in the lives of others and transform them into the leaders they have been chosen to be! Your Self-awareness will make you so aware that you will want others to be the same! It's time for you to influence others and be a Transformational Leader!

Before we discuss how to use your influence-to-influence others, I first want to know what influences you? I want to know what wakes you up in the morning and motivates you to attack the day. What are you working towards? What goals have you set? What destinations are you seeking? Having the answers to these questions is key to growing in self-awareness.

WHAT INFLUENCES YOU?

According to the Merriam-Webster dictionary, influence is the *power to change or affect someone or something.*

Influence is one of those words that we don't hear a lot. We often hear the words motivation, consistency, drive, passion, values, & purpose, but influence not as much. However, influence operates in our lives every day and can come from anywhere. You can be influenced by your friends, teachers, social media, religious beliefs, or an inspiring coach. Still, now I would like to discuss how our lives are influenced by our emotional responses to situations we face daily.

Have you ever asked someone, "Why are you so emotional"? Or have you ever been around a young lady crying but doesn't know why? It's probably because their emotions have overwhelmed them that they responded through tears.

See, we all respond to our emotions differently in different situations. Some people express their disappointments through anger or violence, while others isolate themselves and shut down. Some people express their happiness through gratefulness and joy, while others are more subtle and contained. I share this point to show you how everyone involved was influenced by the same emotions but displayed them through different responses in all these examples. And not one of them was wrong! How you feel is how you feel, but the trick is to respond to your emotions in the best way that will yield a positive response for you and those around you.

After finding out about my parents' divorce, I was devastated and angry for multiple reasons. I didn't know whether to be mad at my mom, dad, or myself. Somebody was to blame, so I responded to my pain by isolating myself from my mom and using the drumline as an outlet. At this point, the pain of my family status was my influence, and I utilized whatever I could to medicate the pain. Remember, self-awareness is being able to reflect on ones' feelings, desires, and behavior. Therefore, I was able to identify my feelings, which led me to desire peace, resulting in the positive conduct of using music as an outlet or form of therapy.

This is important because there will be some giants you face or may have already encountered that will push you to the brink and make you feel like life is turning upside down. For instance, the sudden death in the family, the emergence of COVID-19, virtual schooling, a sudden breakup, losing a scholarship, not being accepted by the desired school, going on academic probation, not being accepted by the preferred peer group or any other situation. These moments are often unexpected and catch us off guard. However, asking ourselves the following questions that we will dive into in Chapter Four during these situations will help us get through these challenges and master our ability to influence others. The questions are:

1. What's really happening?

2. How does it make me feel?

3. What can I gain from this?

4. What can I do with this?

<u>Managing your Influence!</u>

You would be amazed at how many people love and admire you. There are people in your class, home, neighborhood, church, club, or group who watch what you do and desire to be like you. Remember, influence is defined as the *power to change or affect someone or something*. Reading this definition, you may be thinking that you're not trying to change or affect anyone. You may not be waking up every day desiring to be a world changer, civic leader, school spokesman, or shining light, and that's ok. *However, you must know that your ability to change and affect someone's life is not your decision; it's theirs!* Therefore, once you begin to influence someone's life, you become a leader and hopefully a transformative one.

I love talking about this because I can remember when I started to notice that my life was influencing people, and I was beginning to stand out. When I was asked to play significant roles in elementary school plays, play drum solos in music class, and even race in playground field days. I remember times in middle school, not being popular but always asked to make beats on the desks with pencils or play basketball in the neighborhood. Going into high school, though I was quiet, people loved to be around me and were drawn to me. I wasn't really outgoing, but I wasn't shy; I was stuck in the middle. I was quiet when I needed to be but talked when I needed to. I just loved having fun and making everyone feel good, and people admired it. See, my goal was not to be a leader or influence people; I was just myself, and people respected me for it. So here goes your first lesson towards becoming a Transformational Leader...

Lesson #1: Be yourself

If you ever want to get anywhere in life or reach your fullest potential, BE YOURSELF! Have you ever heard this before? I'm sure you have, but this is one of the hardest things to do. The reason being is because there are so many competing voices that we hear daily trying to influence and persuade us to be things that we're not. I dare you to pull out your phone and swipe up through any of your social media accounts. I guarantee that you will begin to compare or second guess your life or the way you are despite your intentions. Three main things affect us from truly being ourselves: comparison, doubt, and overthinking!

- Comparison- the act of looking at things to see how they are similar or different

- Doubt- to be uncertain about (something), to have no confidence in (someone or something)

- Overthinking- to excessively believe that something is true, exists, or will happen

These three things are enemies to your success and will hinder your ability to be yourself and the leader you've been called to be. See, it's hard to be yourself when you're constantly comparing yourself to somebody else. Wishing that you were as tall as them, or as smart, had long hair like them, or hung out with the friends they have. It's hard to be yourself when you doubt your abilities to perform, lead, set the trend, pass a class, or be elected for a significant position. However, it's even harder to be yourself when you overthink everything. You can never truly make decisions in peace or see a new opportunity as one that could be beneficial. Overthinking creeps into our friendships and affects our ability to receive and give love. It often makes us protect ourselves even from those who have our best interests at heart.

So how does one become more self-aware and be themselves? You can start by establishing the following things:

1. Values (What you find meaningful or essential! Principles that guide your life, decisions, and relationships.)

a. Example: One could value faith, creativity, fun, family, and quality time. Another could value resilience, learning/education, security, trustworthiness, love, & order." Values are your core influences that drive your passions and decisions. Once you identify them, you will be able to better manage your today and plan for your tomorrow.

2. Goals (What you desire to accomplish in the future)

a. Example: Some people have fitness goals, relationship goals, financial goals, educational goals, or career goals. These are desired future outcomes that one is willing to work towards to accomplish.

3. Passions (What do you like to do? What makes you happy? What gives your life or energy?)

a. Example: For some, it is playing basketball, creating websites, studying stock charts, doing hair, running marathons, or creating sermons. These are things that give and add value to your life.

These are just a few things you can start establishing today to help you become more self-aware, and there will be more to come in this book but let's move on to lesson number two....

Lesson #2: Take inventory

While serving in the US Navy, I was a supervisor of a significant supply department onboard the CVN78 USS Gerald R. Ford, one of the Navy's newest aircraft carriers. While doing this job, one of my primary responsibilities was to maintain and track the inventory of parts and materials coming in and going out, and I must say this was stressful. We managed thousands of parts, totaling millions of dollars. If something was missing, it would interfere with the ship's overall mission and ability to operate at 100%. Though this was true for my ship, it is also true for us! If you don't know what you possess, you won't be able to operate at 100% and experience the fullness of who you are!

When I say take inventory, you should assess and write down all the good and positive gifts, talents, character traits, and beliefs that makeup who you are. This is how you grow in Self-awareness. Take time to write down a "This Is Me" list! Don't be afraid to brag a little bit, be honest and vulnerable. It may be challenging and even a little uncomfortable; however, it will do wonders for your self-esteem, self-awareness, and emotional wellness. So don't allow comparison, doubt, or overthinking to strip you of this moment. Fight off the negative voices and write down whatever comes to your head. It can be one- or three-word responses but no matter what, do it anyway. Don't worry about coming up with a huge list; just focus on getting something on the paper, and over time, your list will grow and develop as you do!

Here is an example of a few traits you can write down about yourself, and feel free to use them if you'd like:

- Smart

- Kind

- Funny

- Handsome

- Peaceful

- Loving

- Pretty

- Strategic

- Planner

- Patient

- One of a kind

- Go-getter

- Creative

- A Force to be reckoned with

As you can see, your list doesn't have to be severe or tamed, be creative and genuinely dig deep because there will come times when you feel like you have no hope and don't deserve a second chance. There will be times when you will fail a class, bomb an exam, break up with a boyfriend/girlfriend, lose a job, be behind in bills, or make a wrong decision and forget who you are. However, taking inventory and writing down this list will give you something to fall back on and encourage you during the bad times. So I challenge you to take inventory and show yourself who you really are. Now let's move on to Lesson #3...

Lesson #3: Purpose is a Journey

"Purpose" is one of those words we hear and talk about but sometimes feel we will never achieve. I know; however, it is attainable and doesn't take long to figure out. Let's first define what purpose really is:

Purpose- the reason why something is done or used: the aim or intention of something; the dream or goal of a person; what a person is trying to do, become, etc.

I place this definition here because I want to take the mysticism out of "Purpose." Your purpose is not some big lofty thing that only the celebrities, doctors, athletes, or Pastors have figured out. Purpose is something that we can discover today and can be perfected. See, you may not know that you're already walking in purpose. Yes, I said it. You are already walking in purpose. Let's look at the definition again. The description says that purpose is why something is done or used, the aim or intention of something. Therefore, let's break these things down and apply them to your life by asking a few questions:

1. What's the purpose of you going to school every day?

2. What's the purpose of you choosing the major you chose?

3. What's the purpose of hanging out with the friends you hang out with?

The answer to those questions is your purpose and influence for doing those things. See! I told you, you're already walking in purpose and power. But the purpose of this book is to encourage you to be intentional about why you do what you do and help you choose to pursue things that will positively impact your life and those around you.

See, you don't know who is surviving because you keep staying. You may not know who is only living because you keep living. You may not know who will come to class because you continue to go to class. Therefore, I challenge you to take your life seriously and understand that your purpose is more significant than passing a course. It is more important than getting that degree, attaining that scholarship, getting that job, finally getting married, or buying that house. Your true purpose is to accomplish those things while inspiring others to do the same. Your true purpose is to be selfless and vulnerable about your wins and losses and help others meet or exceed your accomplishments. Your true purpose is for you to be yourself, take inventory, and go on the journey of pursuing your goal because it doesn't come overnight. But, if you positively invest your days, someone will benefit from it, appreciate your efforts, and choose to fight towards their purpose.

This leads me to our final lesson of this chapter which is Lesson #4...

Lesson #4: Maximize Every Opportunity

Have you ever heard the phrase, "GO BIG OR GO HOME?" This is a phrase that denotes that a person, when given an opportunity, should give it 100% whether they get another chance or not. You can see this mentality in performers like Chris Brown and Beyonce and athletes like Lebron James, Russell Westbrook, Ja Morant, Steph Curry, Julio Jones, Serena Williams, Michael Phelps, and Simon Biles, Shirly Anne Frasier-Pryce, and even Usain Bolt. These are some of the top performers in their areas of interest, and they became that way because they always give 100% of their effort when it is time to perform. They never slack, take days off, or make excuses, and most of them would be contenders for the race of being the Greatest of All-time. However, I must share that it is not their performances that make them great. It is not the Monday night football games, basketball playoff games, Wimbledon Championships, arena concerts, or Olympic trials that make them great. It is the constant training done beforehand that makes them great.

Maximizing Every Opportunity doesn't start when the lights are on, millions of people are watching, or the people have paid for their tickets. Maximizing the Opportunity begins when you're at home studying, on the field practicing, reading that book, researching for that paper, searching for that job, or seeking out scholarships. Maximizing every Opportunity often comes in times of seclusion and isolation.

Like right now, it is currently June 11, 2021, at 10:48 p.m., and I am on board my ship, which is currently out to sea. I currently have less than 3 months left in the military. Still, I am writing this book to bring inspiration and instruction to you. Nobody around me is telling me to do this, and to be honest, no one cares, but I do! I care about your life! I care about your well-being; I care about your future. Do you want to hear something crazy? We may never meet! However, for the probability of this book being able to change your life, I'm sacrificing time and sleep to create something that will benefit you and those around you.

This is the type of maximizing opportunities I'm talking about. Because if you're going to grow in self-awareness, you will have to sacrifice for it and put your best foot forward. You will have to grind it out and figure out what's really important. There is greatness on the other side of your decision to commit to the journey. You have to maximize the opportunities presented in those quiet moments alone. Because those moments at home, in your room, at school, in the car, or with your friend will determine If you walk in purpose or somebody else's, You choose!

Transformational Leadership Theory

The Transformational Leadership Theory was first coined by James MacGregor Burns, author of the book "Leadership," wherein he draws a contrast between Transactional & Transformational Leadership. Transactional leadership is based on rewarding someone after completing a task. Wherein Transformational Leadership is more about equipping and guiding the focus of the one being led towards the desired goal. This leadership style is usually found in the corporate world and influential organizations. Still, I'm going to apply this leadership style to your life. Michael Cafferky, author of the book "Management: A Faith-based perspective" writes, "Leaders demonstrate transforming leadership when they help others accept the group's purpose." He then writes, "They encourage others to look beyond self-interest to the group's interests. They pay attention to the emotional needs of others and consider individual differences. They also help others become better and develop as people". Why is this important to you?

I wrote this book to inform you that for you to have the life you truly want, you will have to go get it! You will have to take accountability, ownership, and responsibility for your life and its results. No one will give your dreams, goals, or aspirations to you! You'll have to work for it, grind it, cry for it. You're going to have to sacrifice for it, and though these things are true, I need you to have that same mindset towards those around you. Our world is not getting better and crazy things keep happening, so we're all we have! I need you to be the transformational leader who looks out for the less fortunate, bullied, and ridiculed. I need you to be that transformational leader who uses their voice to encourage instead of tear down. I need you to be the transformational leader that takes ownership of the classroom and sets the tone for love, respect, and unity. I need you to be a leader who wants better for yourself and others who don't like it. That's what transformational leaders do. Is this going to be a tall task? Heck yeah! However, you can do it! Leadership is in your DNA. You can't run from it. Take what you're going to learn in this book and apply it to your life first, then give it to others so they can become The Chosen Generation they've been selected to be!

You will be introduced to the 6 CHOSEN principles in the upcoming chapters. These principles will help you grow in self-awareness and become a transformational leader. These principles are simple and easy to apply to every area of your life and, if done correctly, will have drastic and immediate results on your life. So, get ready to grow, expand, and be pushed to another level and watch how you begin to change and see yourself differently. Take the time to fill out the "This Is Me" questionnaire and worksheet on the next page before going into the next chapter, where we will be talking about Committing to Character. See ya there!!

CHAPTER 1 WORKSHEET

TRANSFORMATIONAL LEADERSHIP

UNDERSTANDING & MASTERING INFLUENCE

Whether you have been designated as a leader or not, know that you are a leader! Your voice matters, and you have something to say! On this worksheet, you will answer some questions about the information you read in this chapter and fill out a "This is ME" self-awareness list! Enjoy!

According to the Merriam-Webster dictionary, influence is the *power to change or affect someone or something*.

1. Who or what are the greatest influences in your life today?

_____

_____

_____

2. How have these influences affected your life?

_____

_____

_____

3. Do you believe that you have the power to influence others? If so, how do you use your power to influence them?

_____

_____

_____

4. Can you remember a time that you influenced someone in a positive way? If so, please share

_____

_____

_____

_____

5. Can you remember a time that you influenced someone in a negative way? If so, please share

_____

_____

_____

_____

6. Have you ever or currently battle with comparing yourself to others, doubt, or overthinking? If so, explain how it affected or affects your life today?

_____

_____

_____

_____

7. What are some ways that you overcome comparison, doubt, & overthinking?

_____

_____

_____

_____

"THIS IS ME" List

On the lines below, write down a list of positive characteristics, gifts, and skillsets that you have. Be as descriptive and creative as you can. Don't hold back! Example: Strong, smart, creative, beautiful, athletic, etc.

_____

_____

_____

_____

_____

_____

_____

_____

_____

_____

_____

"THIS IS ME" Art Box

In the box below is another way to describe how you see yourself. So, take some time, be creative, and use this space to draw yourself as creative as possible. Try to capture yourself as best as you can! Have Fun!

CHAPTER 2

COMMIT TO CHARACTER

"Be more concerned with your character than your reputation, because your character is what you really are, while your reputation is merely what others think you are."

-John Wooden

One of the most valuable things you can ever possess is a good character. No matter the amount of money, fame, cars, or talent that you may have, your character will speak for you the most. Think about some of the world's greatest athletes, actors, lawyers, artists, and even governmental officials; they worked hard to make it to their levels of success and accomplishments, but some of them are known for far more. Some actors are known for their bad attitudes, athletes known for their negative locker room presence, and artists known for their rude creation tactics, but more recently, we've witnessed the devastation bad character can cause when it enters the white house. Bad Character, if not checked, can not only affect your life and the life of those around you, but it can also affect your future. Therefore, in this chapter, we're going to utilize a short story to focus on building positive character traits while minimizing bad ones to get the most out of your day, relationships, and opportunities.

Here we go AGAIN!

"Brittany, you have such a bad attitude," says Ms. Sullivan, the teacher of Brittany's 11th grade History class, yelling out from the front of the class. Brittany responds with her usual careless eye-rolling, slouched posture, and quiet, muffled remarks while Ms. Sullivan mirrors her actions and continues on with her lesson. This has happened countless times in this class, and her fellow students have grown immune; however, this day, something was different. At a quick glance, looking back over at Brittany, we see her in tears, doing her best to hide them while wiping them as they go down her chiseled brown checks. Brittany is known for being strong, never backing down, and being able to handle her own. Heck, no one has ever seen her sad, weak, or have a bad day; therefore, this was new, and everybody in the classroom was silent. With one tear after the other barreling over her cheeks, and she fights to catch them one by one, it seems that the problem child seems to have a problem herself, and no one, not even Ms. Sullivan knows what to do.

Brittany, Cried!

There are many things going on in this story. Starting off, we see that there is a teacher yelling at a student in front of her class. Not only is she yelling, but she's also saying negative things to her student as if she no longer cares and has given up. We have the other students in the class who have grown immune to the frequent battles between Ms. Sullivan and Brittany and have decided to stop trying to decide to stick up for either one because their efforts never help the situation.

Lastly, we have a student who appears to be a frequent troublemaker in the class who seems to be untouchable, unreachable, and uninterested in the teacher or the class. She's the "problem student" in the teachers' lounge and is known for having a "bad attitude." She has had some run-ins with a few students, and school staff members, and has been written up for disrespecting two other teachers, but this time her response was different. Brittany cried!

These tears will soon tell a deeper story beyond the surface of what has been revealed and may give you more background about who Brittany really is and maybe, why she acts the way she acts. You may even get to peek into the life of the teacher, Ms. Sullivan, and learn more about her other students. So, before we move on, take the time to review the story above and answer the following questions:

Short-Story Review

1. What is your first impression of Brittany and what character traits did she display?

2. Why do you think she cried and tried to hide her tears?

3. From what you know about Brittany so far, would you say that she has a bad attitude? Y/N, why or why not...

4. If you were one of the fellow students in this class, what would you have done?

5. What is your first impression of Ms. Sullivan?

6. Do you think Ms. Sullivan handled this situation properly? Y/N. Whether yes or no, explain why

After answering these questions, please know that no answer is wrong, but as I give you the background story of the fellow students, Ms. Sullivan and Brittany, your answers may change. Let's continue....

Behind the Tears

Brittany was one of those girls that you loved to be around but didn't want to make mad. She was kinda bossy, witty, had a fierce eye for fashion, and was a natural leader. She was like the sister everybody wanted and had the type of personality that drew people closer to her, even those who didn't like her. Boys, oh, boys, loved her. Though she was only 17, she was mature and knew it. She stood a slender 5' 4" and had a slim waist. Though she often questioned her beauty and wondered how she compared with other girls whose bodies were developing faster, she often made up for it with confidence and personality. She taught herself how to do her own eyebrows, kept earrings in her ears, and did her own nails. Her lips were always shining, baby hair was laid, and you could always find her with an iPhone in her hand and headphones in her ears. She was truly one of a kind.

Even at school, she loved to read and was full of spirit. She was the best student at times, led classroom discussions, answered challenging questions, and had the potential to be a collegiate scholar. Believe it or not, Brittany was a top-tier student, maintaining a 3.2 GPA. A few of the school staff and teachers encouraged her to sign up for the school's leadership association, join the cheerleading squad, and even take on the role of mentoring others, but there were also times when Brittany was angry, disconnected, and uninvolved.

During these times, it seems as if her classes would be cold and lifeless. Other students found themselves mirroring her actions, and teachers would prepare for the worst. Nobody messed with her; teachers would talk about her, her peers tolerated her, but at home, things were different.

See, nobody knew what life was like for her at home. Nobody knew that Brittany's parents split when she was in middle school, and her mother was left to take care of her and her two siblings. Due to financial constraints, her mom couldn't afford to buy her new clothes, and shoes, and their family car was on its last leg, so she had to make do with what she had. Because of this, Brittany was responsible for getting up early to feed her little brother and sister and send them off on the bus to school because her mother worked two jobs: one of them being a medical assistant at a local private practice during the day and the other a night shift supervisor for an Amazon distribution center. After getting her siblings off to school, she would walk a mile to school every morning and barely make it on time while trying to do her best to focus on her education. Shoot, by the time she got to school, she was already exhausted but anticipated the walk home from school because that was the only time in her day that she could have peace and time for herself. However, whenever her siblings were asleep, the house was clean, and her homework was done, you could find her snuggled in her bed reading!

Brittany was an avid reader and admirer of all types of fantasy, crime, thriller, and historical books. It's as if these books provided her the opportunity to transport herself into these other worlds in order for her to experience any new reality she wanted. Brittany was smart, a go-getter, and had a huge heart. It just sucked that rarely anybody knew it but her. She was scared to show compassion, make herself vulnerable, get close to others, and open up because she was battling with the feelings of not having her father in her home. She figured if he didn't want to stay around and love her, why would anybody. She took on the burden of her parent's separation as her own and decided that she would never let anybody else hurt her.

Meet Ms. Sullivan

Ms. Sullivan is a first-year teacher and a recent graduate of Spellman College, attaining her master's in educational leadership. As a newlywed to her high school sweetheart, Brian, they were high in love, but adjusting to the new standards of living together and the realities of her new job, and his commitment to his daughter from a previous relationship was starting to put a strain on their new relationship. She knew all of this would be hard; however, growing up in Georgia, she wasn't a stranger to hard work and didn't mind sacrificing in order to achieve her goals, and was not going to let these challenges defeat her. It's because of her resilience and work ethic that she desired to teach and inspire her students to believe in themselves and work hard to achieve their goals, and she was committed to seeing each one of them successful.

The Classmates

Ms. Sullivan's fourth block class was full of all kinds of students. There were class clowns, very smart but quiet students, very smart but loud students, a few athletes, a college committed point guard, two newly transferred Hispanic students who required extra assistance, students who grew up about a block or two from the school, and a few military brats. Needless to say, to have such a diverse class as the last class of the day would be challenging for anybody. However, though they were so diverse, the kids jelled. They found a way to embrace their differences and appreciate their uniqueness and very seldomly got into fights. Overall, they were good kids!

After reading and understanding the back story of all the characters, take the time to answer the following questions:

1. Has your opinion about Brittany changed since you know more about her? If it has, or has not please explain why

_____

_____

_____

_____

2. Is Brittany's behavior more acceptable now because of her experiences at home?

_____

_____

_____

3. Do you think Ms. Sullivan's attitude towards Brittany would change if she knew what was going on at her home?

_____

_____

_____

_____

_____

4. Has your opinion about Ms. Sullivan changed since you know more about her? Do you think her lack of experience as a teacher plays a role in how she manages her classroom?

_____

_____

_____

_____

5. Since you know more about Brittany's classmates, do you think their differences contributed to their response to Brittany's actions? Do you think their inaction and behavior has helped Brittany in developing better character traits?

_____

_____

_____

_____

6. What do you think will happen to Brittany next?

_____

_____

_____

After reading the short story and the background of all the characters involved, let's start discussing the topic of character and relate them to the characters at hand.

<u>What is Character?</u>

As we know, Brittany was a bright student with high hopes of learning and growing but had a problem expressing her emotions and responding to conflict. She often resorted to being dismissive and argumentative when someone would try to correct her and took their words as threats. On this particular day, Brittany was at a breaking point, and the pressure of trying to balance her personal and educational responsibilities was breaking her down. She had nothing to give and was at her last! She needed help!

Some would say to give her a pass because she is going through a lot at home. Others would say to hold her accountable because she is old enough to make decisions for herself and manage her behavior. Maybe this time, we should let her attitude and disruption pass, but what about the other incidents that came before? What about the other outbursts? What about the other classmates who have been affected? What about the teachers? Well, for the rest of this chapter, we're going to discuss the process of minimizing bad character while developing and displaying good character by identifying emotional trigger points, adopting new strategies of communicating, and helping others to grow in good character as well.

Therefore, whether you find yourself being like Brittany at times, standoffish like the students, or even stressed like Ms. Sullivan, you can commit to good character, overcome bad character traits, and live the purpose-filled life you have chosen to live. Now let's begin!

Character- the way someone thinks, feels and behaves: someone's personality.

Have you ever been around someone who had such a bright personality that their personality made you smile? On the flip side of that, have you been around someone who had a negative personality, and you found yourself being negative?

See, one thing to learn about character is that character is contagious. I'm going to say that one more time, _character is_ _contagious_. _Character starts and is birthed from our thoughts, but they_ _are displayed through our actions._ It's kind of like the game _"hide and_ _seek." Our true character is often hidden until we feel comfortable_ _showing who we really are._ Think about how the world is today! Everybody is doing the same thing, wearing the same things, listening to the same music, and doing the same dances. This is not because the songs, clothing, or dances are always dope, most of the time, these things are not as good as they seem, but because the majority of people accept them, others do as well. So is the case for character!

Do you remember seeing those videos on YouTube where kids were cussing at or disrespecting their parents? It's all over the internet. All types of teenagers and little kids find it funny to make their parents mad and get a kick out of being disrespectful. Side note: I'm going to tell you right now, my mama would've whooped my butt if I tried half of the thing's kids are doing today, but I digress. Kids these days are going crazy, you may even be having your own crazy moments, but I want to ask you: What makes you do it? What do you think is making these kids act the way they do? Were they raised this way? Were they trained to be disrespectful? Are they really this bad? You know what I think? I think that most kids act out in these ways because they are trying to get the approval of other kids. _I think_ _because they struggle with low self-esteem, they are willing to disrespect_ _those that they love in order to get likes from people that they will never_ _meet._

See character is not a fancy topic to write about! It's not something that you hear a lot about on the radio, but it is the foundation upon which all of our lives exist so it is a must that we talk about it now in order for you to attain the best life that you have been chosen to live. As the definition says, character is displayed in how a person behaves especially through their personality. If you could describe your personality in a few words, how would you describe yourself?

_____

_____

_____

_____

Reading over your answer, would you say that you described yourself in a positive way or a negative way? Would you say that you described your personality based on what you think about yourself, on what others say about you, or is it a little bit of both? No matter how you answer these questions, I want you to know that character comes from within!

<u>Character Comes from Within</u>

One of my favorite books says, "So as a man thinks in his heart, so is he..." This means that our thoughts determine who we are and what we do. Our thoughts are the most powerful things that we possess, and if we aren't careful, the way we think about ourselves will interfere with what we do in our lives. Committing to character is not just about watching how you act, what you say, and who you hang around. Committing to character starts with watching what you think about yourself. Think about times when you are around a girl or guy that you really like, applying for a high-paying position, taking a class for the second time, or even trying to pass a midterm exam. *It is during times of challenge, lack of comfort, or uncertainty that our true thoughts about ourselves come out.* Therefore, as we *Commit to Character*, the first thing I need you to do is to understand that character comes from within, and you have the ability to start improving your character by thinking positively about yourself and affirming yourself during times of doubt, uncertainty, and failure.

<u>The power of borrowing Character!</u>

Back in the early 2000s, I was a young teenager in Georgia. The summers were hot, school was out, and I was ready to have some fun. I was a good kid, raised by my mother and father, in a middle-class neighborhood next to the Fort Benning Army base in Columbus, GA. Our neighbors were mostly military, the kids were friendly, and we lived not too far from the city of Atlanta. Things were going well, but at that time, *I was searching for something and didn't know what I was looking for.* To be honest with you, I didn't know what I was missing. It was like I had an empty spot within me that needed to be filled, and I was on a journey to fill it. So, I found myself wanting to go out more, hang out more, and chill with my friends. Though I didn't have many, there were a few guys in my neighborhood that I played basketball with that were a part of a local gang. See, I was never gang material because I had never fought or desired to fight, but because I was cool with them and they were my friends, I figured what the heck.

So I found myself trying to be a part of the gang without being a part of the gang, lol. I figured, if I just wore their colors, played basketball with them, and spoke to them at the local parties, I would be okay, and that's exactly what I did. I borrowed their dress code, mannerisms, hand signals, and attitude. I was officially a non-member of the Southside gang. Before you judge or laugh at me, I was not willing to let them beat me up just so I could wear black and white every day, but let's stay focused. I borrowed their behavior because their behavior seemed to bring safety, security, acceptance, love, and brotherhood. Their behavior seemed to bring them popularity, attention, independence, access, and resources, but at what cost? I knew deep down on the inside that that lifestyle was not for me, but because I wasn't comfortable in my own skin and was battling with insecurity, lack of self-awareness, acceptance, and brotherhood myself, I sought it all outside of my house.

In my case, I was borrowing character in a negative sense, but it can also be borrowed in a positive one. Think about the people you admire, heroes, and role models that you look up to. What is it about them that draws you to them? Is it the way they execute their plans, speak on a microphone, play on a court, design a building, write their books, treat themselves, dress, serve others, build their teams, love their parents, or look out for others? Good character is easy to find and is all around you, you just have to look for it. So, as you're in your stage of development, don't be afraid to act like those that you admire until you develop your own. Shoot, I love Obama, Martin Luther King Jr., and even Kevin Hart. I admire what they stand for, how they do what they do, and their ability to believe in themselves, so I borrow their confidence as I'm building my own, and over time, I no longer need to lean on them because I've developed a positive view of myself because my character comes from within.

Good vs. Bad Character

Identifying good or bad character can be hard for some and easier for others, however, breaking them can be even harder. Have you ever heard that it takes 21 days to break a habit? Well, imagine trying to break the habit of eating chick-fil-a every day. Man, those chicken sandwiches are good! Ok, let's stay on topic. Breaking bad character traits can often feel impossible; however, with intentionality, hard work, and some help from others, breaking bad character traits and implementing new ones can be possible and influential. So, below are a few steps you can take to break bad character traits and implement good ones. And at the end of the chapter, there is a spot for you to complete this exercise.

1. Identify your bad Character traits

a. You may need a little help with this one because it's hard to see yourself without justifying your actions, so ask a friend, family member, teacher, or coach to help you write your list. Don't be upset with what they say, and encourage them to be honest because the more honest they are with you, the more you can overcome and grow from.

2. Identify the results of these traits

a. Identifying the results of your bad character traits is important to break them in your life. If you realize that your inability to trust is pushing your friends away, affecting your ability to have lasting relationships, and hindering you from pursuing your goals, it may make you want to do something about it. If you realize that your trait of procrastination is causing you to gain weight, struggle with low self-esteem, lose opportunities for employment, hinder your GPA, and prevent you from saving money, you may think twice about it.

3. Replace the Bad Positive trait with a Good one

a. Now that you've identified the bad, positive traits and the results they have in your life, now I want you to write down the good character traits or behaviors that you're going to implement to replace them: For example, if one of your bad traits was not trusting others, you can replace it with trusting those in your family and close friends then branch out to others. If one of your bad traits was procrastination, you could replace it with assertiveness or proactiveness. If one of your traits was laziness, you could replace it with diligence and accountability.

4. Write a strategy of how you're going to implement these new traits into your life and implement them immediately

a. Since you've replaced the bad traits with good ones, now it's time to write down a strategy of how you're going to implement them in your life. For example, if your new trait is proactiveness, your new strategy could be: Instead of waiting until Sunday night to complete your assignments, you will now complete and turn in your work no later than Friday evening. If your new trait is trust, your new strategy could be: Instead of pushing people away for fear of being hurt, I will get to know people and embrace them with kindness until I feel that my values are being challenged, and I will walk away.

Therefore, to conclude this chapter, I want you to know that nobody is perfect and that everybody is working on making themselves a better person. Whether you are young, old, black, white, in high school, or college, we all are striving to be the best people we can be in order to have a lasting impact. Therefore, remember that character is a decision and can be cultivated over time. Character can be groomed, nurtured, and enhanced by consistent effort and the willingness to progress. If you really want to grow and commit to character, I challenge you to ask those around you to help you. I challenge you to ask your best friend, boyfriend, girlfriend, fiancé, or spouse to help you commit to character and grow as a person. Not only will it make you better, but committing to character, it will also enhance your relationships. When people see that you are serious about yourself, they will be serious about you. They will help you in any way they can and encourage you to grow, so never forget that there are people watching you and are rooting you on to be the chosen leader you've been called to be!

<u>What about Brittany?</u>

Brittany actually is doing great, and she is now one of the go-to students in Ms. Sullivan's seventh block class. See after that class was over, Ms. Sullivan pulled Brittany to the side and apologized for her actions.

She said that she never should've spoken to her that way and didn't mean to make her cry. Brittany, though timid and reluctant at first, picked up her head and apologized as well for her actions. She explained that she wasn't crying because of Ms. Sullivan. She was crying and upset in class because this would be the third night in a row that she would be home by herself with her siblings without her mom. This would be the third night that she would have to take care of them, feed them, help them with their schoolwork, and do her own.

See, her attitude was never with Ms. Sullivan. Actually, she would be disgruntled in her class because she knew when the bell rang, she would have to leave. Brittany felt more love in Ms. Sullivan's class than she ever did at home, but because she was unsure of what she felt and how to communicate it, she reacted with anger and frustration. It turns out that she actually loved Ms. Sullivan and Ms. Sullivan was a great teacher. They were well on their way to being great friends, and who knows what the future has in store for them both.

CHAPTER 2 WORKSHEET

COMMITTING TO CHARACTER

1. What is the definition of Character?

_____

_____

_____

_____

2. What's the difference between good and bad character?

_____

_____

_____

_____

3. After reading the conclusion of Brittany's & Ms. Sullivan's relationship, what do you think drew them together?

_____

_____

_____

_____

4. Do you think it's equally importantly for teachers and students to walk in good character? Why or why not?

_____

_____

_____

_____

5. Do you believe that you character affects your ability to lead others? If so, what type of leader do you desire to be?

_____

_____

_____

_____

6. When Brittany was defiant in class, was she a good example or a bad example?

_____

Good vs. Bad Character Breakdown

Here is the time to write down what you read about during the chapter. Take your time and be as honest as you can because your results are based on your honesty. If you need help, feel free to grab a partner to help you through the four stages:

1. Identify your bad character traits:

_____

_____

_____

_____

2. Identify the results of your bad character traits:

_____

_____

_____

_____

3. Replace bad positive traits with Good traits:

_____

_____

_____

_____

_____

4. Write down your plan of action:

_____

_____

_____

_____

_____

_____

_____

_____

_____

_____

_____

_____

_____

_____

_____

_____

_____

_____

CHAPTER 3

BE <u>HONEST</u> ABOUT YOUR PRIORITIES

"If it's a priority, you'll find a way. If it isn't, you'll find an excuse."

-Jim Rohn

Have you ever felt like there is not enough time in the day? After going to school, doing homework, managing bills, applying for jobs, cooking, and cleaning up, there is often not enough time for you and the things that you love to do. Well, I must tell you, you may be right. Often, there won't be any extra time for you to take care of yourself, relax, hang out with friends, or have fun because you may not correctly prioritize your life and responsibilities. In the world that we live in today, prioritizing is one of the hardest things to do. With the competing distractions of social media, TV, Netflix, and many other forms of entertainment, it truly feels that our time is being stolen from us and given to tasks that don't add value to our lives. However, the truth is that we have the power to take control of our lives, seize our time, and prioritize what we care about to gain the best benefit for ourselves and others. Therefore, this chapter will focus on teaching you how to identify and utilize your priorities to increase your effectiveness as a leader and help others do the same. Let's Begin!

<u>What is a Priority?</u>

Priority- the things that someone cares about and thinks are important

Identifying your priorities are essential to your personal life and your ability to lead others because they provide the framework for you to work in. They are so important that your priorities are leading and guiding you every day, whether you know it or not. For example, if you value education, it will show up in your study habits. If you value friendships, it will show up in the amount of time you spend with them. If you love being accepted, it will show up in the amount of time you invest in pleasing others. Therefore, one of the first ways to identify your priorities is to determine what you think about the most.

I've been saying that I want to have a nice body with a 6-pack. I've signed up for multiple gym memberships, turned my garage into a gym, and purchased equipment, yet I still don't have a 6-pack, and I feel uncomfortable taking my shirt off at the beach, lol. It may seem funny, but the truth is, I don't have a 6-pack because my body and health are not a top priority to me. No matter how much I try to tell myself that fitness is a top priority, my body shows me otherwise. See, it's not that working out and fitness is not a priority of mine; it's just not a top priority. Therefore, identifying your priorities is one thing, but ranking them from greatest to least significant is different.

Ranking priorities at your age and stage of life will put you lightyears ahead of those who don't. As you get older, you meet different people who will have big goals, dreams, ideas, gifts, talents, and abilities but won't become as successful as they could simply because they didn't correctly prioritize. Have you ever met a fellow student in your class who was super smart but super dumb at the same time? Like they're smart for no reason, just naturally brilliant, but at the same time super lazy. Or you may know someone who is super athletic but hates to practice or another who can ace a test without studying. Their natural abilities are extraordinary, and they're able to achieve great things, but the truth is, if they prioritized excelling in their natural abilities, they could be even more successful.

Therefore, as we continue in this chapter, I want to help you discover your priorities by diagnosing what you care about. Let's look back at the definition of priority:

Priority- the things that someone cares about and thinks are important

Now let's move on to the short story:

Meet Robert and RJ!

Robert is a sophomore at Bethune Cookman College in Florida and is 20 years old. A native of Norfolk, VA, he is far from home but excited to be on a new adventure. Robert graduated high school in 2019, earning three academic scholarships, a band scholarship, and the opportunity to go to school for free and make a spot as a member of the mighty marching wildcat band. His first year of college was a bit challenging as he learned how to manage his free time, course load, band practices, and personal time, but throughout the year, he managed well and still maintained a 3.0 GPA.

In anticipation of his second year, he took a trip back to Virginia to visit his family, church, and high school and participated in community service. He cared about these things, and he couldn't wait to get home to share his college experiences. Robert volunteered as a junior counselor at a local community center, where he loved to work with youth. He also had fun working with the other volunteers. The summer was going great and was almost over, but he met a young boy named RJ.

Roderick was his name, but everybody called him RJ. RJ stood around 5'6", was skinny, and had dark brown skin and beautiful white teeth. His legs were super long; his knees were always ashy. He loved to wear shorts and could always be found with some anime t-shirt. RJ was one of those kids that you loved to be around. He always had a smile on his face and had the biggest personality, but you couldn't help but recognize that he often wore the same clothes throughout the week. He would come in some mornings, anticipate the camp breakfast, and go throughout the day to ask for snacks. RJ was a great kid, but you could tell something wasn't right.

After sitting down to speak to RJ, Robert found out that RJ's father had been laid off from a local plant in the area and his mother worked at a local restaurant that was downsizing because of the Covid-19 pandemic. RJ's father worked odd jobs here and there, and his mother, who had an associate's in culinary arts, put in applications for multiple restaurants but hadn't yet received any responses. Though this was the case, RJ never wore his disadvantages on his sleeve. He found a way to keep on smiling and made sure everybody around him smiled.

After finding all of this out, Robert was hurt. He went home that day, and couldn't get RJ off his mind. He talked to his mother and friends about him, and he couldn't figure out why he felt the way he felt. It was as if Robert felt an obligation to do something about RJ's situation. He had to do something. Robert couldn't just let RJ keep wearing the same clothes, could he? He couldn't just let him be picked on, could he?

See, RJ reminded Robert of himself when he was younger. He and his mother didn't always have a lot, and his father worked hard, but even with his parents' combined incomes, they still had troubling times. Therefore, because Robert was once in RJ's shoes, he had compassion for him and wanted to make a difference in his life. *Though Robert was young, he cared for people and wanted everybody to be cared for.*

After saying his nightly prayers, Robert got in the bed and laid down. While thinking about RJ, he came up with a plan. Robert decided that he was going to give RJ all of his clothes. So, he woke up early the following day, went to the kitchen, grabbed some trash bags, and filled them with clothes from all of his drawers and closet. After a few minutes of rustling, he woke his mother up. She screamed from her room, "Boy, what are you doing in there?" "Nothing, mama," he said as he continued to take more clothes off of the hangers and throw them into the bags.

After about 20 minutes, his mother sees four trash bags full of clothes, hangers on his bed, and empty shoeboxes scattered on the floor. His room was a mess because Robert's room was usually spotless. He hated having a messy room.

His mom, confused but curious after seeing it all, asks, "Now, where do you think you're going"? "Nowhere, Ma," he says. "I'm taking these clothes to RJ at the Rec. His parents are struggling; he comes in hungry every morning and wears the same clothes almost daily! I'm tired of the kids teasing him, Ma; I have to do something!" Amazed at her son's desire to help, she says, "Okay, but you better not give him all your clothes! And put them new shoes I just got you back in the box and in that closet!" Robert laughs and says, "Ok, Ma," as he puts some of the shoes and clothes back and takes the remaining three bags to work.

With everything packed in his car, Robert goes into the house, kisses his mom on the cheek, and speeds off to work. Getting to the Rec Center early, he parks his car by the front entrance, greets the fellow staff members, hugs a few kids, and waits. It seems like hours go by as parents drop their kids off and race into the facility. One by one, they run by, waving and screaming, "Good Morning Mr. Rob," and he waves back, but he hasn't seen RJ. Looking at his watch and seeing that it's only been 20 minutes, he calms himself down and gets himself together.

As he looks up, he sees a green Honda Accord pull up, stop in front of him, and RJ hops out. Filled with joy and excitement, Robert opens his car door, pops his trunk, and says, "RJ, I got something for you!" RJ says, "what is it?" and follows him to the trunk. As Robert opens the trunk, he pulls out the bags, sets them on the floor, and pulls out some clothes. With RJ looking confused, Robert says, "These are for you!" RJ immediately says, "Whoa, Mom, look!" She hurries around her car, races to the trunk sees the clothes in RJ's hand, and immediately starts crying!

Now, Robert wasn't expecting this. He just wanted to help a kid in need; he didn't know it would be this serious, but RJ's mom looks up, wraps her arms around Robert's neck, holds him tight, and with tears in her eye, says, "Thank you, thank you, thank you. You don't know how much this means to us." RJ then looks up, drops the clothes, and grabs on to Robert as well, thanking him for the clothes and overjoyed with Robert's love. Robert did a great thing that day! He made someone else's life better, but why did he do it?

Short-Story Review

After reading this story, please answer the following questions?

1. How do you feel about Robert?

_____

_____

_____

_____

2. What would you say Robert cared about or held as a priority?

_____

_____

_____

_____

3. How do you think Robert's actions affected RJ?

_____

_____

_____

_____

4. How do you think Robert's actions affected RJ's parents?

_____

_____

_____

_____

5. If you were in Robert's shoes, what would you have done?

_____

_____

_____

_____

6. Have you ever been in a situation like this, if so, what did you do, and why did you do it?

_____

_____

_____

_____

7. Can you see how Robert's care for people led him to help others?

_____

_____

_____

_____

8. Would you consider Robert a leader for doing what he did? Y/N, please explain

_____

_____

_____

Real leaders Care!

Have you ever been around somebody who was always trying to tell you what to do but didn't even know who you were? A teacher who yelled but didn't know your name? A partner who fussed but didn't know the full story? How did these experiences make you feel? There is a difference between being corrected by someone who cares about you and somebody who doesn't. This is why leadership is crucial because leadership is not all about being in charge of people. Leadership is about showing others that you care.

Take Robert, for example. Did you ever read in the story that he yelled at RJ, accused RJ of wrongdoing, or disciplined him? We didn't even read that RJ did anything wrong, caused problems, or disrupted the camp. In our story, Robert saw RJ in need and cared enough to do something about it. That's the central theme of this story and this chapter! So, let me ask you, will you care enough to do something about it? Will you care enough about your family to make it better? Will you care enough about your future to do something about it? Will you care enough about your health to do something about it? Will you care enough about your education to do something about it?

I'm writing this book to kill the *"I Don't Care"* mentality! Yes, the *"I DON'T CARE"* mentality. This mentality is one that many students adopt when they are uncomfortable, uncertain, or feel like a task is impossible to do. This mentality shows up in times of great promotion, opportunity, and advancement. This mentality shows up in relationships, family circles, and even friendships. It's usually a default defense mechanism used to protect oneself from being hurt or disappointed.

This mentality is usually a cover-up from previous trauma, so when trying new things or assisting others in similar situations, we adopt this mindset to keep ourselves from losing the little that we still have left. I understand how it feels to be angry, upset, and disappointed. I know how it feels to be unsure, afraid, and doubt if I could be successful and achieve great things. I understand how it feels to be hurt emotionally, abandoned, talked about, cast aside, overlooked, and feel unappreciated. Believe me, I know; however, harboring these feelings towards yourself and others and adopting this mindset may seem like it's protecting you from being hurt, but it's really becoming a prison, preventing you from being truly happy and being the best person, you can be. It stops you from giving and receiving love even when you want to and prevents you from trusting others who have your back.

One of the most significant signs of possessing an "I don't care" mindset is always pushing people away, never getting close, or making yourself free. Sometimes, you may be mean on purpose, then feel bad later or get close to people only to end the relationship prematurely. However, if you're living like this, you can be free and be the whole person you have been chosen to be because there is great work for you to do, and you are worth fighting for. Millions of people are waiting on you, and the world is yours, so keep on fighting and tear those prison walls down.

Tear the Walls down

You are way too valuable, talented, smart, gifted, and called to be in the prison of your own fear. There is too much in you that the world needs. There is too much in you that your family needs. There is too much in you that your friends need to be trapped within! So I challenge you to say the following affirmations out loud:

1. I am Valuable

2. I am Strong

3. I am Special

4. I am Chosen

5. I am Important

6. I am Needed

7. I am a World Changer

8. I am not my Past

9. I will succeed

10. I am a Leader

11. I am Enough

These are more than words; these are declarations. These are more than words; these are affirmations that will become your reality. See, the prison walls that we spoke about before can be torn down if you say these words constantly over yourself. All of the great, wealthy, and influential people that you know of today practice the act of speaking positive words over themselves because they understand that words have power. They know that sometimes you have to talk yourself into a place that you're not in at the time. Doing this show's that you care about yourself, love yourself, and want better for yourself. This will turn your life around and position you to see the need in others and help them turn their lives around, just like Robert did. Robert was able to change RJ's life and his whole family's lives as well.

What do you care about?

At the end of this chapter, there will be questions you will answer that will help you identify your priorities, but for now, we're going to start the discussion about discovering your own. Again, this is important because whether you believe it or not, your life is already driven by your priorities; therefore, change your priorities if you don't like the way your life is going. You must answer the questions below because what makes you cry, laugh, mad, hurt, and inspires you exposes your priorities. For example, despite being raised in a single-parent home, I would ask my mom if other students could come to stay with us because I knew they lived in bad situations. They would live with us for months at a time and be a part of our family, which made me happy. Therefore, my priority or what I care about is: helping youth to live their best lives. I focused on it daily and did my best to ensure that everyone around me was doing good, which automatically made me a leader.

See, being a leader doesn't start when you are made a leader. Being a leader begins the minute you start influencing others. And people only follow those that they feel care about them; therefore, whether you are in high school college, have a lot of friends, or few friends, a student leader, team captain, or not. You have Influence!

I'm going to say that one more time, you have Influence! So let me ask you this question, will you take on leading!

Lead with Priorities in Mind

Taking on the responsibility to lead can be a big deal and something that we're not always ready for or even expecting. In Robert's case, at the beginning story, he didn't plan on giving his clothes away when he came home for the summer. He didn't plan on giving his clothes away while going to work every day. However, when presented with an opportunity to make a difference, he took it! He seized the moment and changed somebody else's life.

Leadership is not always about a position or title you hold; leadership is mostly about your ability to influence or change someone's life for the better. However, sometimes leadership can be an inconvenience. Sometimes we're forced to lead in our homes at early ages, take care of a grandparent, babysit younger siblings, get a part-time job while trying to finish our degree, lead a group of friends to do better, or even take control of a class project. Though this can be the case, leading with priorities in mind is essential and will benefit you in your leadership success.

So, let's go back to the previous chapter, where we learned about committing to character. Committing to character is a foundational principle to remember as you enter leadership in any capacity because there will be times when situations will test your character. Come on, think about it. Think about when a fellow student was getting on your nerves, but you decided to stay calm. You know what you were doing at that time; you exercised self-control because you held peace as a priority. Think about when you had a major paper due by Sunday at 11:59 p.m., and you turned it in at 11:58 p.m. You were exercising resilience to complete and turn your paper in on time because you prioritize good grades. Think about when your girlfriend or boyfriend was fussing at you, and you decided not to cuss them out. You were utilizing patience because you prioritized your relationship. However, to truly commit to your priorities, you must first commit to character because it is your character that will drive you to follow through on the things you are committed to.

Therefore, your leadership journey will be a long one of learning and experiences. Somedays you're going to enjoy it and you won't. Somedays, you're going to be proud of your accomplishments, and other days you won't; however, we all are doing our best. Honest about your priorities will help you as an overall person.

As you discover and rank your priorities and the things you care about, you will begin to experience an easier life and one of greater productivity. Your schedule will even be more balanced, and your relationships will grow rapidly. Establishing priorities helps you to create boundaries for your life and even vet your relationships.

If someone or a group of people doesn't align with your newly established priorities, permit yourself to find new friends who align with your priorities. If you are in a relationship with someone who doesn't align with your priorities, permit yourself to find someone that does because if you don't, you will end up angry and bitter towards that person when it was your job to separate yourself from them. In all, you have what it takes to be a transformational leader.

Establishing and ranking your priorities makes you a better person and a better leader equipped with a strong influential voice that will encourage those around you to be leaders as well. I'll see you in the next chapter as we get *Open about our Emotions*!

CHAPTER 3 WORKSHEET

HONEST ABOUT YOUR PRIORITIES

Please take the time to answer the following questions on the lines below. This exercise aims to discover what you care about through common scenarios that we face daily. This process is not only crucial towards identifying your priorities, but it is essential for starting the process of ranking them and implementing them in your personal life.

On the lines below list a few things that make you mad.

_____

_____

_____

_____

On the lines below list a few things that make you happy.

_____

_____

_____

_____

On the lines below list a few things, people, or places that inspire you?

_____

_____

_____

_____

What are 3 things that you care about the most in your life?

_____

_____

_____

If any, what thoughts keep you up at night or are constantly on your mind throughout the day?

_____

_____

_____

_____

_____

_____

_____

On the lines below write down the top 5 things that you care about.

_____

_____

_____

_____

_____

_____

_____

_____

_____

_____

_____

Priority Ranking List

On the lines below, take the time to rank your priorities. This will be a great way for you to properly define your priorities and rank them by importance. There is no wrong answer. As you complete this portion of the worksheet, you will develop the ability to bring more structure to your life. Use this information to create a daily, monthly, or yearly schedule, or to decide what things in your life you want to keep or put off until later. (Ex. Education, health, financial stability, mentorship, employment, career placement, relationship, friendship, creativity)

1. _____

2. _____

3. _____

4. _____

5. _____

Daily Schedule

Use your priority list to fill out your daily schedule on the lines below. You can use this daily schedule to ensure that you are intentionally scheduling times throughout your day to invest in your priorities. If you value health & wellness, studying, reading, spending time with your family, or meditation, use the lines below to set aside times throughout the day to focus on those priorities and increase your success in those areas.

<u>Time</u> <u>Action</u> _____

_____ to _____ :

_____

_____ to _____ :

_____

_____ to _____ :

_____

_____ to _____ :

_____

_____ to _____ :

_____

_____ to _____ :

_____

_____ to _____ :

_____

_____ to _____ :

_____

_____ to _____ :

_____

_____ to _____ :

_____

CHAPTER 4

BE <u>OPEN</u> ABOUT YOUR EMOTIONS

"Emotions can be the enemy. If you give in to your emotion, you lose yourself. You must be at one with your emotions because the body always follows the mind."

-Bruce Lee

Have you ever been asked, "Why are you so emotional?" or told, "Get out your feelings"? I've heard these statements on TV, in movies, on social media, and especially in music. Some people even have "in my feelings" playlists. It's okay. You probably have one, lol. However, it does speak volumes about the apparent existence of emotions within us all. See, being emotional is not bad. Getting angry is not bad. It gets bad when we allow our emotions to rule us negatively. For example, there is nothing wrong with being mad about someone who disrespects you as long as you don't respond out of your anger. However, emotions are essential to our lives and given to us as indicators of our existence. Still, the more we try to compress them, the more we go against our nature and hinder ourselves from the inside out. Therefore, this chapter focuses on helping us identify and embrace our emotions and gain the courage to express them confidently to others.

I'm in my Feelings!!!

In 2018, Drake, one of the all-time greatest rappers, in my opinion, came out with a song titled "In my feelings." This song topped the charts, and the world gravitated to it as it expressed the feelings he had for a particular young lady named Ki Ki. Ki Ki, was not showing him any love or attention, and he was working hard to get her back, but it wasn't working. Then in 2021, another great artist, Jasmine Sullivan, produced a song titled, "Pick up your feelings." In this song, she writes to a guy she no longer dates. She thoroughly expresses that he needs to come to pick up his things and feelings from her house. Their relationship was now over, and she no longer wanted anything to do with him. Both of these songs have catchy choruses, and the artists are incredibly talented, but their songs are centered around the mistreatment and damage of their emotions.

These songs aren't singing about love in a good way. These songs express the pain that comes from having feelings and sharing them with others, which is why this chapter is essential. But first, what is an emotion?

- **Emotion**- a strong feeling
- **Feeling**- an awareness by your body of something in it or on it; emotional state

After reading these definitions, what are some of your daily feelings or emotions? Would they be joy, happiness, fear, anxiousness, grief, excitement, love, motivation, feeling overwhelmed, angry, lonely, peaceful, or isolated? If so, it's normal because we all experience these emotions and must learn how to manage them.

One of the greatest examples of managing emotions is when you must manage them in front of someone you like, are interested in, or admire. You know what I'm talking about! When they come around, you get all nervous, start sweating, and forget what you want to say. You feel the butterflies in your stomach and sometimes begin to laugh uncontrollably randomly. For boys, when we are around beautiful girls, we say random things that don't make sense. She'll say, "Hey," and we'll say something like, "What's up lil mama?" Bruhhhhh, who says "lil mama?" And girls, when a cute boy comes around, he'll say, "What's up," and she'll start laughing and act like she's tough. Nevertheless, in moments like these, we try to control ourselves, but often our emotions get the best of us. Therefore, since we aren't able to live without our emotions, we must be honest that we have them and be able to communicate how we feel.

Meet Brianna

"Jessica, Let's go, we're going to be late, and you know Brandon is going to be there tonight!" says Brianna. He is a sophomore in her class that she has a crush on. He invited her out to a fraternity party. "Girl, I'm coming. I have to fix my eyelashes", says Jessica, screaming out from her bathroom. Jessica and Brianna are college roommates at Howard University and childhood friends from Baltimore, Maryland. They met when they were younger, went to high school together, and are now Freshmen at Howard. Brianna is a half tomboy, half girly-girl, an all-star softball player for Howard's girl softball team, has a big personality beautiful smile, and stands around 5' 9". Some people say that she looks like Gabrielle Union, but she constantly denies them and says Gabrielle has nothing on her.

Jessica, on the other hand, is the complete opposite. She is quiet, loves to read, is an educational scholar, and strives to hide her figure by wearing oversized clothes and sweatpants. She's what one would call a bookworm and doesn't like being around many people. However, somehow, Brianna convinced her to come out to the party and be with her as she tries to impress her new friend Brandon. So, Jessica decides to put on some nice fitted jeans, a pair of vans, a halter top, and a Jean jacket. She comes out of her bathroom, and Brianna is amazed. "You need to show that body off more often. You could get a man tonight if you weren't so mean!" Brianna says to Jessica as she grabs her keys and walks towards the door. Jessica reluctantly smiles and says, "Girl, shut up! I'm not like you. I don't need a man. How many guys do you talk to anyway? Isn't he like the fifth one?" Jessica then grabs her phone and follows Brianna to her car.

When they get in her blue 2014 Honda Accord, a used car her father bought her a few months before they left for college, Brianna puts on her seat belt, pulls out her phone, and texts Brandon saying that she's on the way. He responds, saying, "I can't wait to see you!" As Brianna smiles from ear to ear, Jessica looks over and says, "Can we go?" sternly puts on her seatbelt and pulls out her phone.

See, Brianna's upbringing was pretty good. She grew up in a middle-class neighborhood, and her parents worked good jobs. She loved them. She and her dad were like best friends, and she and her mother were like peas in a pod. She was their only daughter, and they decided not to have any more kids. No one knows why. Her father was a middle manager for a financial firm. Her mother was an executive director for a local non-profit in the Baltimore area. They had been married for 15 years, and they both had successful steady careers. They worked hard to send Brianna off to college, and now that she was out of the house, they were sure to be married for 15 more years.

By the time they pulled up to the party, it was already 10:30 p.m and the party had been jumping for about an hour. Stars were lighting up the night sky. Cars were everywhere, boys were walking around looking at the cute girls, and the girls were prancing around, strutting with confidence, knowing that the boys were checking them out. There were many people outside of the house and a few couples lounging around the porch and the front yard. Even before they got out of the car, you could hear the music blasting and the bass booming down the street. This was their first college party, and it looked like it would be a great night. After finding a parking spot and removing their seatbelts, you could see the anticipation in Brianna's eyes. Jessica looked at her and said, "The only reason I came to this party is that you asked me to, so you better not leave me." Brianna looked over and said, "I'm not going to leave you, girl. You know I wouldn't do that." "Whatever," Jessica said, and they headed to the front porch.

Pulling out her phone, Brianna texted Brandon, letting him know she was outside, and they stood on the front lawn waiting for him. After a few seconds, he met them at the bottom of the steps. Brandon was a cool guy. He was studying to be an Engineer, was intelligent, well-spoken, tall, handsome, and had nice wavy hair. Brandon had recently pledged a fraternity, became a new member, and wanted to celebrate with Brianna. He walks up with a big smile, gives them both a hug and asks, "What took y'all so long? I thought you weren't coming." Brianna immediately glanced at Jessica, and she starts laughing. Excitedly, they finally decided to go inside and see what the party was really about!

As soon as they step inside, there are people everywhere, and there is hardly room to walk. The girls are dancing, boys are standing on the walls, couples are sitting on the couches, and the DJ is killing the music. There were hot wings on the kitchen table, pizza in the dining room, and a cooler full of alcohol right in front of the DJ booth. This was a real college party.

Immediately, Brianna grabs Brandon's hand, and they rush to the dance floor and start dancing. Song after song, they are attached almost seamlessly as the music flows through the atmosphere. Brandon can't keep his hands off her, and Brianna can't keep her hands off him. The two were one. Brianna does the very thing she said she wouldn't do. She leaves Jessica, who was standing by herself between the bookshelf in the living room, and a couple won't stop kissing. Continually, guys come up to her, asking to dance, but she denies them and continues to stand there with her arms folded. From the outside, she looks mean, intimidating, and uninviting, but on the inside, she really wants to enjoy herself and dance, but she just can't do it. She wants to enjoy herself, but she's afraid. She doesn't want to be rejected. She can't dance like those other girls, or can she?

An hour goes by, and more people join the party. People keep coming out of nowhere. The house is truly over capacity, so Jessica decides to step outside and use her phone and takes Brianna's phone with her. While she's standing outside, scrolling through Instagram, she notices that Brianna's phone won't stop ringing. She pulls it out and see's that Brianna's father has called her five times, and it's almost midnight. So, she goes inside, taps Brianna on the shoulder, and shows her the phone screen. Brianna quickly leaves Brandon inside and jets outside to figure out what's happening. With all types of thoughts and scenarios going through her head, she finally gets on the front lawn and sees that not only has her father called her five times, but he also sent her a text message. Brianna unlocks her phone, goes to her messages, opens his thread, and sees a message from her father that reads, "Your Mom is in the hospital." She immediately panics and calls her father to see what is going on. After three rings, her father answers the phone, and she says, "Dad, what's going on?" he replies by saying, "I don't know yet. The doctors just took her into surgery! It's not looking good!"

Short-Story Review

1. While reading this story, what emotions did you feel and did they change throughout the story?

2. Were there any characters in the story that you could see yourself as? If so, please explain why

3. How would you describe Jessica's emotional state and personality?

_____

_____

_____

_____

4. How would you describe Brianna's fathers' emotional state?

_____

_____

_____

5. How would you describe Brianna's emotional state before she arrived to the party?

_____

_____

_____

_____

6. Why was Jessica so afraid to dance with boys at the party?

_____

_____

_____

_____

7. Why do you think Jessica was so focused on studying and covering up her body?

_____

_____

_____

8. How would you describe Brianna's emotional state after she received the news from her father?

_____

_____

_____

_____

Identify your Emotions

Identifying your emotions is essential for living and progressing as a transformational leader. Whether you are a high school senior, mother of two, middle child, an A-student, junior in college, or hoping for a promotion, you will have to manage your emotions every day. As you can see in the story above, emotions can change at any moment. Sometimes you can wake up feeling like you can conquer the world, but there are other times that you feel hopeless. Sometimes you feel like working out and getting your health together, but there are other times that you decide not to work out and order a whole pizza for yourself. Therefore, we must identify how we feel so we can manage them in a way that brings us ultimate fulfillment, productivity, and peace of mind.

To communicate honestly and be open about our emotions, we must first Identify that we have them. The authors of the book _Emotional Intelligence: Current Evidence From Psychophysiological, Educational and Organizational Perspectives_ discussed this point. They state, "To perceive emotions is to accurately identify emotional content in one's own and others' faces, voices, gestures and other modes of information gathering" (Raz, Sivan, Zysberg, Leehu, 2004).

So many times, due to past experiences, rejection, or trauma, many try to turn off their emotions to protect themselves. They believe that acting as if they have no emotions will prevent them from being hurt again, but this is far from the truth. This posture hurts us and makes us numb to the joys and cares of life. However, we are alive and blessed to have feelings to experience and are able to communicate them to others. But sharing how we feel can be easier said than done.

Having the courage to speak up requires confidence and humility and often makes you vulnerable. Do you like feeling vulnerable or putting yourself out there before your friends or loved ones? I know I don't, but I've learned that it's necessary to identify how I feel and communicate them to others because communication fuels my relationships and yours.

Daily, you are constantly inundated with opinions, voices, and influences. Whether you are in class, attending virtually, scrolling through social media, hanging out with friends, or relaxing with your family, we constantly receive signals that trigger emotional responses. For example: have you ever walked into a house and smelled some excellent food from the kitchen or received a good grade from an exam you've previously taken? How did these moments make you feel? Good and happy, right! See, the thing is, we're not always able to control our emotions, but we can control how we respond when they are triggered.

Managing your Emotions

Do you remember that student with a bad attitude in chapter 2? She was considered "the bad student" and was talked about by students and faculty. She was looked down upon by senior leaders and was judged by her actions. This judgment all took place because of how she was responding to her emotions. This is important to understand because we often blame others for things that go wrong in our lives. But we must look at how we respond to them to see our role in the situation. If a teacher gives us instructions that we don't like, it's not our job to lash out or rebuttal. If a parent corrects us, it's not our job to be argumentative. If a coach disciplines our technique, it's not our job to rebel. When situations like this arise, our job is to assess the situation, identify how we feel, and respond respectfully. In times like these, I like to ask myself the following four questions:

1. What is really happening?

2. How does it make me feel?

3. What can I gain from this?

4. What can I do with this?

These four questions give me a systematic process to help me navigate emotional mazes that I may go through and help me see situations from proper perspectives. You can implement these four questions in times of stress, depression, defeat, or failure. You can also use these questions in times of achievement, success, breakthrough, or triumph.

Now let's break these questions down one-by-one by using two scenarios:

1. What's really happening?

This question is crucial in times of stress, confusion, anxiety, disappointment, uneasiness, let down, failure, mistake, or sadness. It causes you to focus on what is really happening or has happened, apart from your feelings about it. Here are two examples of how to answer this question:

i. What's really happening? (Scenario #1)

1. David, a freshman at BTW High School, lives in a single-parented home with his mom and two sisters. He and his father don't have a very stable relationship, but his mom does her best to nurture and provide for them.

1. ii. What's *really happening? (Scenario #2)*

1. Kayla, a junior at Discover University, studied tirelessly for an upcoming exam but failed, causing her course grade to drop dramatically.

Note: Now, as you can see in both scenarios, there were no emotions involved, just pure facts about what was really happening. This is important because it is extremely easy to fabricate or make up something that didn't really happen. Therefore, in Scenario #1, we can see that David lived in a home with his mom and two sisters. We know nothing about his father's whereabouts nor his feelings concerning the matter, but we can learn the facts by answering the question.

In Scenario #2, Kayla worked hard to study for her exam, but she still didn't pass. This doesn't make her dumb, stupid, or unable to pass the class. It just means that she didn't pass the exam.

Now let's continue with questions 2 through 4, utilizing the two scenarios that have been presented:

2. How does it make me feel?

This question may be a little hard for some to answer because it will require you to be vulnerable, honest, and able to express your emotions. Newton's Law says that every action has a reaction, and I believe that is true with our emotions. So, look at these two examples and see how the students in the examples answered them:

i. How does it make me feel? (Scenario #1)

1. Sad because I wanted my parents to stay together to maintain our family and disappointed because they are no longer married. I'm angry because they should've done better and confused because I wonder if it was my fault.

ii. How does it make me feel? (Scenario #2)

1. Disappointed in myself and a little worried that I might not be able to bring my grade up to a passing status before the semester is over.

Note: Do you see how in both scenarios, the students were able to be open about their emotions. Being able to do this will bring clarity and healing and strength to overcome the situation at hand.

3. What can I gain from this?

This question causes you to look past what happened and how you may feel to focus on what you can gain from the situation. It's not that what you feel isn't real, or your emotions aren't necessary, but a part of managing your emotions will come from finding a positive in the midst of pain.

i. What can I gain from this? (Scenario #1)

1. Understanding that things happen in relationships but knowing that my parents would never do anything to hurt me intentionally, nor themselves. Secondly, understanding that everything will work out for our family, and just because they are no longer married doesn't mean that we're no longer family. Finally, I developed compassion and patience for both my parents because life is too short to hold resentment toward those that I love.

ii. What can I gain from this? (Scenario #2)

1. Understanding that failing an exam doesn't mean that I'm a failure. I tried my best and put my best effort forward. Even though I didn't pass, I decided to continue doing my best and seek assistance when I needed it. I recognize that I am capable and intelligent.

4. What can I do with this?

This question puts you in a position of leadership and influence. Having the courage to answer this means you're willing to take your experience and share it with others. Once you can acknowledge what happened, identify your emotions, and figure out the lesson, it's time to share it with others. It's time to tell your story. It's time to be a transformational leader.

i. What can I do with this? (Scenario #1)

1. I can help other students who are going through similar situations cope and channel their emotions positively while teaching them ways to communicate them. I can also teach them how to use compassion to support their parents and not blame themselves for their separation.

ii. What can I do with this? (Scenario #2)

1. I can start a study group, bringing students together to help each other prep for major exams and class assignments. I can also use this failure to start a podcast on how to manage and overcome challenges in college.

As you can see, going through these four questions will do wonders for your life and help you grow as a person and a leader. Emotions are the most challenging things to understand at times but can also be the most potent guide. They can be so confusing yet so understood. Therefore, as a student, son, mother, freshman, or CEO, we have to be willing to be honest about how we feel and communicate those feelings to others.

There have been so many things that I wish I would've said. I wish I said "yes," or I would've said "no." I wish I would've said I wasn't ready, or I would've said I was, but I was just afraid. I wish I had the courage to speak up for myself or challenge others who disrespected me. I wish! These are not thoughts or regrets that you want to live with, but now, you have the tools necessary to cycle through your emotions to help you communicate how you feel. Don't be afraid to use your most powerful weapon because you have the power of life and death in your Tongue! Your voice can either lift people up or tear them down! Your voice is powerful and can speak things into existence. Now it's time to be serious about your future and speak it into existence now. I'll see you In the next chapter!

Chapter 4 Worksheet

Open about your Emotions

How comfortable are you at communicating the following: 5 being very comfortable, three being somewhat comfortable, and one not being comfortable. Please circle your level of comfortability on a 1,2, 3,4,5, scale:

1. Successes: 1 2 3 4 5

2. Failures: 1 2 3 4 5

3. Secrets: 1 2 3 4 5

4. Fears: 1 2 3 4 5

5. Accomplishments: 1 2 3 4 5

6. Dreams: 1 2 3 4 5

7. Goals: 1 2 3 4 5

8. Disappointments: 1 2 3 4 5

9. Desires: 1 2 3 4 5

10. Faith/Beliefs: 1 2 3 4 5

1. What were your top 3 levels of communication?

_____

_____

_____

_____

2. What were your lowest 3 levels of communication?

_____

_____

_____

3. Why are you so comfortable being open and communicating your top 3 choices?

_____

_____

_____

4. Why are you less comfortable being open and communicating your lowest 3 choices?

_____

_____

_____

5. Do you believe fear, rejection, and abandonment affects your ability to communicate your emotions? If so, how has it affected you in the past?

_____

_____

_____

6. If there was one area of your life that you would like to be more open about, what would it be and why?

_____

_____

_____

_____

CHAPTER 5

BE *SERIOUS* ABOUT YOUR FUTURE

"Education is our passport to the future, for tomorrow belongs to the people who prepare for it today."

-Malcolm X

"Man, I can't wait to get out of this house!" This was a thought that I used to have when I was growing up and that you may have also had. This phrase stemmed from a desire to go beyond my parent's home and into a future of my own, but truthfully, I just wanted to go and experience the exciting possibilities that the world had to offer. See, high school was excellent, but I was ready to go to college. I was prepared to attack life and make way for myself. I was ready to be grown and on my own, but now that I'm grown, I want to go back and be a kid again, lol. When I was younger, I assumed that the future would be easier, more fun, and unpredictable. I assumed that the future would be more glamorous, adventurous, and full of fun and crazy experiences.However, though this is true, it does not always start or remain that way because if you're not careful and don't properly prepare yourself today, your future will suffer and won't be what you desire it to be. Therefore, this chapter focuses on developing a future-focused mindset and teaches you some strategies to prepare for it and lead others to do the same.

What do you want to be when you grow up?

How many times have you been asked this question? Personally, I was asked more times than I could count. However, I looked forward to answering it because I loved the response that those who asked would give me. When I would respond by saying, "I want to be a Doctor," or, "a Lawyer," or "I'm going to be a Dentist." I would say these things because I saw how important these people were and the lifestyles they lived, but the truth was, I didn't know what it took to become them. I was simply saying these things to make my mother and others happy because there's nothing like making your mother, father, or guardian proud. They love it when we say things they agree with and choose paths they desire for us, but what happens when our desires don't align with their desires for our lives.

What happens when your mom desires for you to run track, but you want to play basketball? What happens when your father wants you to be a football star like he was in high school, but you want to act in Hollywood? What happens when you want to go to an HBCU(Historically Black College & University), but your parents want you to go to an Ivy League institution? What happens when they say not to date a person, but you love them anyway? What do you do? I decided that my life and my future were my decision, and to reach my future goals, I would have to be *serious about my future.*

Let me start this off by saying I'm not saying to disregard your parent's feelings towards you; what I am saying is that their wisdom and guidance will be the foundation upon which you make your daily decisions. Even if you live in a single-parent home with your grandmother, are raised by a neighbor, or have come up through foster care, you too should value the voices of the adults and leaders in your life. Their life experiences have taught them a lot and given them wisdom beyond their years. Their job is to ensure that you live the best life you can possibly live. Their job is to prepare you to be successful and prevent you from making the mistakes they may be made growing up. Therefore, to *be serious about your future*, you should want to have influential voices involved in your life and give you input on your future decisions because adulting is not easy or fun sometimes.

So what do I mean by being" *serious about your future?*" I mean that you will have to be intentional about making your future goals a reality today. You will have to decide to put in the work today to see your success tomorrow and define what success is to you.

This is a big statement because my definition of success and your definition of success can be two different things. Success to me is that I am debt-free and financially stable, while success to you may mean committing to a degree plan and graduating on time. Therefore, to truly be serious about your future, you must first define what success is and means to you. On the lines below, take the time to explain what success means to you. We're going to do this now because this will be the foundation upon which everything in your life is built. This definition will guide you and help you keep track of your progress as you pursue your desired future. Go ahead and write down your definition below:

Success:

_____

_____

_____

_____

_____

_____

This is so important because it will give you something to do and go after. Whether you are a high school junior or graduating with your master's degree, you can be busy but not progressive if you don't have aim. I'm going to say this way. You can be busy but not better. You can be accomplishing things and getting things done but still not be going anywhere. If you don't have a vision, you will likely perish; therefore, maintaining your vision and goals during times of setback is essential to gaining your desired success. About maintaining vision, Michael Hyatt, author of the book, *The Vision Driven Leader: 10 questions to focus your efforts, energize your team, and scale your business,* writes, "When slowdowns and setbacks threaten to throw you off course when breakthroughs remain elusive, vision can sustain the mission and lead you to your projected outcome" (2020, p.52).

It's just like a treadmill; people spend hours on treadmills every week only to run in place. They can change the speeds, incline, and even verify their heart rate, but after the walk or run is over, they still haven't moved from the place that they started. Therefore, to prevent you from doing that, understanding what success means to you from the beginning will give you a reason to work to see your future come to life amid the adversity and challenges you will face!

The Trail of Tears

When I was growing up, I learned about an event in American history named the "Trail of Tears." The trail of tears was a journey that Cherokee Indians had to take from the Southeast area of the United States to the West due to forced immigration. Their homeland was no longer safe, and they were forced to relocate somewhere else, dismantling their businesses, property, rights, land, and claims. With no direction, little resources, and strength, this group of people journeyed into the unknown, hoping to relocate and resettle themselves in a new place that they could call home. There were many obstacles; they often ran out of food, were overtaken by illnesses, and perished from a change of weather. Family members were separated, and they lost many years of heritage and history. However, some survived and made it into new grounds and started new lives for themselves and their families through it all.

I place this history lesson here because I believe it truly depicts how the process of reaching our desired future is in a real way. See, accomplishing your future goals is possible, but I must tell you that they will not be easy. In order to truly become who you desire to become, you must be resilient!

Resilient- able to become successful again after something bad happens

See, resilience is not something you can buy or borrow from your friends. Resilience is not something you can learn from watching a YouTube video or reading a book. Resilience is a character trait often developed during times of challenge, and you may be able to think about moments in your life when you had to be resilient. Maybe you've had trouble in school, relationships, or your career. You've had a hard time mastering your schedule, appetite, desires, or focus, and it was during these times that you had to utilize a resilient mindset. Therefore, I say: "So what if you failed an exam? So what, you missed a deadline? So what, you didn't get the scholarship. So what, they picked someone over you. These things happen; however, life is not over, and I need you to bounce back. Remember, resilience is defined as being able to be successful again after something bad happens. It's a mindset, and it's the mindset you're going to have to adopt to be *serious about your future* and successful in it also!

So, I dare you to say out loud: I AM RESILIENT! I WILL NOT QUIT, I WILL NOT GIVE UP, I WILL NOT GIVE IN, I WILL BE SUCCESSFUL! You know what, let's change that last statement and make it present tense and say out loud: I AM SUCCESSFUL!!

See, the secret is that success is not an event. Success is a mindset. I'm going to say that one more time: Success is not an event; success is a mindset. Therefore, the sooner you can understand this, the sooner you can become the transformational leader you've been chosen to be! Transformational leaders understand that focusing on the future will cause you never to achieve it. I know you've probably never heard that before but focusing on your end will cause you to never reach it. You could be so focused on graduating from college that you forget to file for financial aid. You could be so focused on studying for an end-of-course exam that you fail to pass a class. You could be so focused on getting married to the right one that you neglect your friends today. Therefore, the true secret to being *serious about your future* is to manage your days, one day at a time.

Managing your today is way more important than worrying about tomorrow because tomorrow has enough problems of its own. As a leader and influencer, your job is to manage your days as if there is no tomorrow because somebody is waiting on you to be you so they can be them. I'll say that another way! If you don't dare to be you today, somebody else won't have the courage to be them tomorrow. See, I don't think you understand how important you are! Your importance has nothing to do with what you have or possess. Your influence stems from who you are. It's your character, personality, and compassion for others. The way you serve and go out of your way to help others. The way you light up a room and fill it with joy. That's something that somebody will need today, so don't be discouraged that you're not where you desire to be right now. Focus on how you can make an impact where you are until your reality and fantasy look the same!!

Meet Me, Robert B. Vann

On April 22, 1989, I was born in good ole Savannah, GA. Georgia was a great place to grow up, but I loved visiting my family in Alabama on the weekends. So, during the school year, I would stay in Georgia and go to school, but I would be in Alabama with my grandparents during the summers. Columbus, Georgia, where I grew up, was a beautiful city about 2 hours outside of Atlanta, GA. It was thriving with life but small enough not to have major traffic. Weekly, you had the option of walking along the beautiful Riverwalk, attending a local college football game, enjoying a major concert, hockey game, or house party. However, in Eastaboga, AL, the only things we could do were go to the one gas station, grocery store, or post office in town. If you had a license and a car, you could even drive 30 minutes outside the city to the one movie theater or city mall. It was the country where my grandfather left us 40 acres of land and little to do, but I used it to my advantage.

While I was there, my imagination would go crazy, and I found myself building and crafting all types of things. I learned how to fish, went hunting with my uncle, and tried to build a four-wheel bike out of some scrap wood and old bike tires. My grandfather taught me how to catch worms with two steel pipes and even turned a riding lawnmower into a go-cart. I'm telling you, life was good. All I could see and think about was the moment, and I never thought about the future or what it would look like. However, as time progressed and I entered my junior and senior years of high school, I had to figure out what I was going to do with my life.

So, I went back to the drawing board and decided that I would go to college to be a band director. I made this decision because I had been in my high school band during my first and second years and couldn't see myself doing anything else, and this wasn't a hard decision to come by. I say this because I decided to play basketball during my 10th-grade year, and anyone who knows me knows that I love to play ball. So, if you want to play me one-on-one, let me know!! However, during my 10th-grade year, I decided to play basketball and made the team. Junior Varsity that is, but I made the team, and I was excited. As the season started, we practiced and played against other teams, and I wore my jersey with pride. Nobody could tell me anything! Shoot, I was the man until I noticed something. I barely got to play. My coach would put me in the game to replace the starting point guard with 2 seconds left on the game clock. It was embarrassing and shameful, and I didn't understand, but now I do.

See, I didn't get to play because I wasn't committed to the game. I wasn't committed to practicing hard on my own or watching game film. The only thing I was committed to was putting on that jersey and showing out for the girls. I didn't really want to work hard, I just wanted to be seen, and you can't be successful at something just because you want to be seen. You must be committed to the process. You must be willing to prepare! What am I saying? Preparation breeds success!!

However, at the end of the season, my mother asked me if I was going to play basketball again the following year or stick to playing in the marching band, and what do you think I had decided to do? I decided to commit to the band and quit playing basketball, and my decision paid off. Because of the decision I made in 10th grade, I benefited from it during my senior year. I graduated with a 3.27 GPA, earned an academic and band scholarship, and attended Miles College in Fairfield, Alabama, marching for the mighty Purple Marching Machine Band.

I share my story because everything I'm telling you to do in this chapter is everything that I had to do growing up and even in my life today. I had to decide what I wanted to be, establish my definition of success, and be willing to sacrifice and work hard to get it. I had to work hard to build my craft and maintain my grades. I had to work hard to commit to practicing my drum and leading my drumline. I had to work hard to focus on my education while maintaining big dreams for myself. But in all, it worked out for me because I was *serious about my future* and was willing to prepare for it.

The 5 P's (Prior Preparation Prevents Poor Performance)

"Failing to prepare is preparing to Fail." – John Wooden

I wish I could tell you how necessary preparation is to your future. Preparation is key to making your dreams a reality, but it often yields no results. Prior preparation prevents poor performance is more about who you become during the preparation process than what you're preparing for. Preparation is more about the character you develop than the position you will possess. Yes, it's going to be great when you graduate, get married, start that business, and get hired. Feel free to celebrate, but the real celebration should be when you sacrificed your sleep to study to pass that midterm. The celebration should be when you sacrifice time with your friends to stay home and work on your business plan. The celebration should be when you sacrifice eating that good food at the family reunion and stick to your diet. Preparation is not all about what you're preparing for. Preparation is about who you're becoming while waiting on your big opportunity. However, while you're preparing, you need to expect separation.

You may not want to hear this, but when you decide to be serious about your future, development, or welfare, certain people are not going to like it. I'm sorry I must tell you this, but some of your friends may not like the fact that you want better for yourself. See, it's easy to live and settle when everyone around you is settling and comfortable, but when one person in the crew decides to do something better, those around you may get uncomfortable. Those around you may challenge and ask you questions about why you want to change? Do you think you're better? Or do you have what it takes?

Some may even say that you won't succeed, are nothing, or will never make it out, but I challenge you to harness your inner resilience and say that you will succeed no matter if they're with you or not.

If you find yourself being challenged by people around you for desiring to change or be better, put yourself around people who are positive or are doing the things you wish to do. Put yourself around positive voices, mentors, or leaders who will push you to be better. Put yourself around friends who want to go to school, learn, grow, and develop. Put yourself around people who are excelling in your areas of influence so that you can understand their ways and adapt their methods because if you do this, you may not only be successful but exceed your imagination.

Being able to separate from others may be challenging, but it's even harder to break away from yourself! It's even harder to break away from your bad habits, mindsets, actions, and routines. It's hard to separate from old perspectives of negativity and limiting beliefs, but It's even more challenging at times to believe in a prosperous future. Therefore, as we end this chapter and you continue to prepare for your future, I need you to work hard on separating from yourself. I need you to be honest and take inventory of the things about you that are holding you back. There's no reason for you to be blessed with a lot of money if you have bad spending habits. There's no reason for God to bless you with a new girlfriend or spouse if you are struggling with trusting others and jealousy. The time between now and the future is for preparation and working hard to become the right person to handle the success. It's on you to prepare and be serious about your future because nobody is going to do it for you.

You have what it takes, and somebody is waiting on you! Be *serious about your future* and be willing to *Earn to Own*! I'll see you in the next chapter.

Chapter 5 Worksheet

Serious about your Future

Many people like to ask about your 6-month, 1-year, 3-year, 5-year, and 10-year goals. Well, this worksheet is going to help you establish your goals. Write them out in a simple and practical way. Have Fun!

Your goals are derived from your values and priorities, so don't be surprised if your goals line up with your previously stated priorities in Chapter 5. For this portion, take the time to use your imagination and write out how your life looks a year from now. Write it as if it's a year from today.

1 year from now: "Yo Rob, the last year has been crazy! You've sold over 10 thousand books and have been able to travel the nation, empowering students to be transformational leaders. You've been featured on local radio and news stations and have an opportunity to partner with Eric Thomas and Inky Johnson. Your business has provided 3 other people with great jobs, and you met a beautiful woman you are engaged to. You all are planning to get married around October of 2023! Life is good, and I'm proud of you, bro, Keep grinding!

Now, this is my example, so on the lines below, take the time to be creative and write a quick letter to yourself:

1 Year from now:

_____

_____

_____

_____

_____

_____

_____

_____

_____

_____

Now, I want you to do the same two years from now! On your mark, get ready, set, and go:

Two years from now:

_____

_____

_____

_____

_____

_____

_____

_____

_____

_____

I hope you had fun with these two imaginative experiences because your future will be comprised of what you dream of today. Now, on the lines below, break down your 1-year vision into some practical goals that you can set and monitor on a monthly basis and answer why these goals are important to you—understanding the why behind your goal is essential because there are going to be days that you don't want to work towards your goals. Still, your ability to remember the reason why you are pursuing your goals will motivate you to keep following them. So, Let's focus on three main goals that you desire to accomplish over the next 12 months and build a strategy to complete them.

1 Year: 3 Main Goals

Goal 1:

_____

_____

_____

- Why is accomplishing this goal so important to you?

_____

_____

_____

_____

Goal 2:

_____

_____

_____

- Why is accomplishing this goal so important to you?

_____

_____

_____

_____

_____

Goal 3:

_____

_____

_____

- Why is accomplishing this goal so important to you?

_____

_____

_____

_____

_____

Steps to Completion

During this step, on the lines below, your job is to write down the steps needed to accomplish your goal. For example, if your goal was to lose 20 pounds. Your steps could go as follows: workout four times a week, replace all of my carbonated beverages with water, only eat fast food on the weekends, meditate and write in my journal for at least 15 minutes a day, and hire a fitness coach. As you can see, the yearly goal is attainable, but it's our job to define the steps needed to accomplish these goals. Therefore, take the time to go through all three goals and establish the steps required to complete them on the lines below. If you don't know the steps, feel free to reach out to others and ask them for assistance. This will help you gain accountability and encourage others to assist you in completing your desired goals.

Goal 1

Step 1:

_____

_____

_____

Step 2:

_____

_____

_____

Step 3:

_____

_____

_____

Step 4:

_____

_____

_____

Step 5:

_____

_____

_____

_____

Goal 2

Step 1:

_____

_____

_____

Step 2:

_____

_____

_____

Step 3:

_____

_____

_____

Step 4:

_____

_____

_____

Step 5:

_____

_____

_____

_____

_____

_____

_____

_____

Goal 3

Step 1:

_____

_____

_____

Step 2:

_____

_____

_____

Step 3:

_____

_____

_____

Step 4:

_____

_____

_____

Step 5:

_____

_____

_____

Now that you've established your future goals and defined your steps to complete them go after them with all your might and watch your life transform as you become a Transformational Leader.

ROBERT B. VANN

CHAPTER 6

EARN TO OWN

"You can't have a million-dollar dream on a medium-wage work ethic."

- Unknown.

There is a saying that hard work pays off, which is so true! For some, working hard comes naturally and is a part of their everyday lives, but for others like me, I have to work hard, to work hard. Okay, let me say that again, often, I have to work hard, to work hard. What I mean is that I have to be intentional about the work I do and how I do it. For example, if I desire to finish a major research paper, I have to be intentional about doing it. That means I have to be intentional about scheduling time out to do the research, set up an outline, find sources, and write my paper. I have to be intentional about getting the work done. See, working hard doesn't always come easy. Often, we either work hard, are lazy, or are afraid of success or failure, which prevents us from working at all. Still, I challenge you to decide to put your all into what you desire to do and be willing to *earn to own*. Therefore, this chapter will discuss the importance of developing an "earn to own" mindset and how to use it to transform your life and the lives of others as a transformational leader.

Work Hard to Work Hard

Imagine it's a cool summer morning, and you've been out of school for about three weeks. You're out of your daily school routine and have grown comfortable waking up any time you'd like. Life is good, and you're looking forward to a day full of adventure. So, you get up, rub your eyes, stretch, yawn, and head to the bathroom. While you're in the bathroom, your mom bangs on the bathroom door and says, "I thought I told you to take that trash out! This is the second week in a row we've missed the trashman." Barely awake, you don't know how to respond, but your immediate thought was that if you were being honest, the reason you didn't take the trash out is because you didn't feel like doing it!

Have you ever been in this position before? Lol. I have! However, this statement may be funny, but the principle of this story can be applied to any situation. So, let me ask you; have you ever been faced with something that you didn't feel like doing, or have you ever passed up an opportunity that you just didn't feel like doing? It wasn't that you couldn't do these things or perform the tasks. You simply didn't feel like doing it. On the surface, this may be an acceptable response for you; however, deep within, this repeated statement exposes an underlying issue that many face daily.

Meet Torres

Torres is a 21-year old freshman at Discover University. He is pursuing his Bachelor of Science degree in Computer Science. He has been out of high school for three years but is now going to college and doing what he wants to do. Torres was one of those that passed his test without studying but didn't care about his future.

School officials loved Torres. They encouraged him to apply himself, work hard, and try harder to become the best student he could be. They would give him tips on leading others and how to use his influence to be a mentor. They would encourage him to seek scholarships, grants, college acceptances, and future possibilities, but Torres decided not to take their advice because he did not care. Torres didn't see the value in going to college. He was just trying to move through high school, so he didn't put forth the effort. Crazy enough, in Torres' senior year, he graduated in the top 20 of his class. His GPA was 3.6, and he graduated with honors. However, though he was one of the top graduates, Torres didn't apply for schools, scholarships, or grants. He didn't want to write the essays required, fill out applications, or send letters because he didn't feel like doing it. So when his fellow students were earning millions of dollars in scholarships, he was left embarrassed. Though Torres was naturally more gifted than others, they were willing to work to get what they wanted and earn it.

Short-Story Review

After reading this story, how would you describe Torres and his character?

_____

_____

_____

_____

Why do you think Torres is this way he is?

_____

_____

_____

_____

What's the biggest difference between Torres and the other students who applied for college and scholarships?

_____

_____

_____

_____

Do you think natural ability is enough to reach your goals? Why or why not?

_____

_____

_____

_____

Is work ethic permanent or can it be cultivated? If so, how

_____

_____

_____

_____

Do you think fear played a role in Torres's "I don't feel like it" attitude? _____

Do you think laziness played a role in Torres's "I don't feel like it" attitude? _____

How has fear and laziness affected your life educationally and personally?

How has fear and laziness affected you as a leader?

If there was any advice you would give Torres to encourage him to be better, what would it be?

You have to want better for yourself!!

Whether you_are in high school or college, you can attain the best things in life. Whether you're striving to earn a college degree, becoming a doctor, getting married, having kids, earning a 4.0 GPA, starting your own business, becoming physically and emotionally fit, growing in your spirituality, or developing your leadership voice. These things are all attainable, but only if you believe they are. See, the things I listed above were all physical; they can be touched, seen, bought, or borrowed. However, are they all that life has to offer? I want to suggest that the greatest things in life are those that money can't buy. The greatest things in life are eternal and hidden deep within yourself. These things are peace, love, joy, and confidence. These things are values, priorities, commitments, resilience, and determination. Earning to own isn't all about working to own things with your hands. Earning to own is also about owning the process of becoming who you desire to be.

Earning to own is about pursuing and sticking to a task you said you would do. Earning to own is about sacrificing for the betterment of others even if it inconveniences you. Earning to own is the key to being a transformational leader and empowering others to do the same. Earning to own is all about becoming more Self-Aware! Somebody has to want something different, bigger, and better. Somebody has to dare to dream and go beyond the status quo. Somebody has to challenge the norm and break the barriers of previous limitations. History is riddled with people who mastered this very mentality.

Take Harriet Tubman for example. Harriet Tubman was a slave who wasn't satisfied with being a slave. She hated it, and though it was legal and accepted by the nation, she never accepted her chains. Let me say that one more time: though she was a slave, had a master, and was bought as a slave, she never accepted her chains. She never accepted being a slave. I hope this encourages you and that, as a result, you begin to apply this same mentality to your life. Remember that she didn't settle, give up, or adopt the "I don't care" attitude we talked about before. She decided that slavery wasn't good enough for her and for those around her.

Somewhere in life, you will have to decide that where you are isn't where you belong and that you will no longer continue to live the way you have been living. You will no longer accept being abused, mistreated, or living in poverty. You will no longer be a subpar student, excel at being average, nor will you continue to stay in productive mediocrity. You have to choose to be better and break out of the chains of yesterday. You have the opportunity to *earn to own*!

Though she was a slave, Harriet Tubman decided that she would not accept being a slave and decided to flee for her freedom. She believed that if she could free herself, she could free others. She was willing to put in the work and she jeopardized her life for the possibility of freeing others. Harriet Tubman was a transformational leader. She is credited with freeing hundreds of thousands of slaves and could've freed more if they only knew they were slaves. It is also said that when she attempted to free slaves, they were not willing to leave their plantations. They were unwilling to take the risk for their freedom. They were content with being slaves. So, I want to ask you:

are you content with the life you are living? Are you willing to do the work to get what you want? Are you lazy?

The Curse for Laziness

Laziness- disinclined to activity or exertion: not energetic or vigorous; moving slowly or sluggish, droopy, lax.

Laziness is the curse to all productivity. It will prevent you from being a top student, best performer, friend, spouse, child, and leader. Come on; you know what I'm talking about. Those times when we are supposed to be writing, but we don't feel like doing it. The times we're supposed to be supporting a friend, and we don't feel like it. We were supposed to be studying for an exam, and we didn't feel like it. These moments are times when we often justify our inactions with some sort of excuse or claim that we will do that task later. Let's be real. How many times in the last 30 days have you thought or said to yourself, "I'll just do it tomorrow?" I'll admit, I say this often, but this statement has prevented me from excelling, and it hindered my ability to progress in my life. In these moments, I chose laziness over my task and made my feelings more important than the task at hand.

I'm sharing this with you because if you truly want to *earn to own* and be a transformational leader, you have to have a strong sense of self-awareness. You have to be honest with yourself and say, "Bruh, I'm lazy." It may not feel good to admit this, but owning this way of life will enhance your self-awareness and your ability to lead in ways that you will never know. See, self-awareness is not all about being aware of what you do right; it also has a lot to do with what you do wrong. Self-awareness is about becoming aware of your character traits, values, priorities, commitments, and how they operate in your life. Therefore, if you truly want to be a transformational leader and know you struggle with this, you must acknowledge that you are lazy or have lazy tendencies. Did you know there is a difference?

See, some people are just flat-out lazy. They don't want to do anything but complain and procrastinate. On the other hand, some people aren't lazy per se but have lazy tendencies. These people have what I call "selective laziness." Those who live in selective laziness like to pick and choose when they will and will not apply themselves. These people aren't bad; they decide to be picky about how they distribute their energy. I'm even guilty of this; however, I've realized that what you accomplish hits differently when you know you worked hard on it! A science project hits differently when you know you worked all night to finish it! Imagine how mad you'd be if you spent multiple hours on a paper, received assistance from the writing center, and turned it in on time, yet your professor tells you that you did a poor job! Would you be mad at your professor or upset because he did not acknowledge your hard work? This is the sole reason for this chapter. I want you to experience the fulfillment of hard work.

There is nothing like the power of finishing! In our society today, everybody glorifies starting, but true success is finishing what you start. Imagine how much you could accomplish in school if you finished what you started? Imagine how much more fulfilling your relationships would be if you finished what you started? How much better would your health or body be if you finished what you started? The people we idolize on Instagram, listen to on the radio, or see on TV aren't famous because they start well. They are famous because they finish well! They get paid millions of dollars because they finish well! They're successful because they finish well.

So, let me ask you, what do you need to finish? It could be a college application, scholarship essay, business plan, research paper, or significant assignment. Maybe you need to finish the conversation you started with your mom, finish cleaning your room, creating your vision board, or designing your new home! No matter what it is, don't rob yourself of the fulfillment of finishing through hard work any longer. Being willing to work hard to earn what you desire is the key to accomplishing any goal and is a decision you can make today. It won't be easy, and life will constantly test your choices, but if you stick to it and don't give up, you will reap the benefits of being willing to *earn to own* and position yourself to *Never Settle*!

CHAPTER 6 WORKSHEET

EARN TO OWN

After reading Torres' story and reviewing the results of his actions, I have a few questions for you:

1. Are you struggling with the "I don't feel like it" mentality?

_____

2. Are there any areas of your life that you could be doing better in if you put in more effort? If so, please explain.

_____

_____

_____

3. As a leader, it's important for others to see you working along with them, do you believe this is true? If so or if not, please explain

_____

_____

_____

4. It is said that leaders lead from the front, however, do you think there is a such thing as a lazy leader? If so, would you be willing to follow them? Why or why not?

_____

_____

_____

5. Looking over your life, would you say that you are lazy, have lazy tendencies, a mixture of them all, or aren't lazy at all? Why are you this way?

_____

_____

_____

_____

_____

6. Often, working hard or trying our best is influenced by our motivations, therefore, what would you say motivates you?

_____

_____

7. Have you ever struggled with your motivation or desire to be successful? If so, why do you think this is?

_____

_____

_____

_____

_____

_____

_____

_____

8. If there was one thing in this world that you were willing to earn to own, work hard to achieve, and sacrifice for, what would it be and why?

CHAPTER 7

NEVER SETTLE

"Are you really happy or just really comfortable?"

-Unknown

Are you happy with the life you're living, the grades you've earned, or the friends you hang around with? What about your health, level of income, or career path? If not, why not? What's keeping you from achieving or living the life you truly desire? Many students worldwide have settled for lives that they are not pleased with. They follow the latest trends, fashion styles, and fads but still don't have peace or feel accepted. However, you can break out of that prison of normalcy and build your own bridge to success and self-awareness. It's your job to dream big and pursue your dreams with all your might. It's your job to see what has already been done and dare to be better. Dare to write a better book, shoot a better shot, build a bigger business, preach a better sermon, enhance a stronger relationship, display greater character, and create more memorable memories. The world needs you to challenge the status quo and create new opportunities, inventions, apps, clothing designs, music, movies, community programs, law firms, churches, and therapy centers that have not yet been seen! This will not be easy, and the tendency to fall back into your routine will be tempting. However, you must push past your usual preferences to receive an extraordinary life.

Therefore, through the implementation of boundaries, standards, and non-negotiables, you will not only grow in self-awareness but position yourself to lead effectively and build a prosperous life outside of the box of normalcy.

The Power of the Word "No"

In my opinion, one of the most powerful words in the English language and not often used is "No." It has the power to tear down an economy, disrupt business partnerships, hinder one's opportunity to go to their desired college, and even end a long-term relationship. But why is it able to do so much damage? When the word no is used, it demonstrates that an individual has a set of standards, boundaries, or non-negotiables. The word no exposes that one has values, commitments, and priorities. It also shows that they are willing to protect themself and those around them. Saying the word "no" can make life better or worse. It can make you happy or sad, and even make your life better or worse. As the quote says,

"I refuse to please others at the expense of my emotional well-being. Even if it means saying no to people who are used to hearing yes." -Anonymous

The most self-aware people can say "No"! No is the new standard. It protects them from unwanted relationships, opportunities, and experiences but is also used to protect them from being hurt. Have you ever been in a situation where "No" could have prevented you from getting hurt or in trouble? I'm sure you have, and you probably regret not saying "No." Good news!

Why don't we say "No"? There could be multiple reasons. Some may have a hard time because they're afraid of being rejected. Others may struggle because they want to be accepted, lack confidence in their voice, or feel they have no reason to say "No," because they have not established their values. Though all of these may be true and evident in some lives, I've learned to start the process of saying "No" and to never settle again.

A great way to start is by establishing boundaries, standards, and non-negotiables. These three components are so important at your age because they will provide the foundation and framework upon which your life and purpose will live. However, your life will become a constant cycle of mediocrity, aggravation, and stress without them. A prison of repeated events and lack the fire to motivate you to pursue greatness. Therefore, for the rest of this chapter, we will be discussing boundaries, standards, and non-negotiables and how to implement them in your personal lives and leadership portfolio. If you do these correctly, your life will change for good, and your self-awareness will go to a whole new level! Let's get it…First stop. Boundaries!

Boundaries

Saying "No" indicates one has a strong sense of self-awareness because it takes courage to say "No." It takes courage to stand up for yourself and choose the opposite of what someone or a group of people desires you to do. It takes courage to say no in the midst of a tempting situation. It takes courage to say no to the past and believe in your future possibilities. It takes courage to say no to generational curses amongst your family and choose to walk in freedom. It takes courage to say no!

Saying "No" is the act of drawing a line in the sand, stating that this is your boundary and you will not cross it. Dr. Henry Cloud & Dr. John Townsend, authors of the book, *Boundaries in Marriage: Understanding the choices that make or break loving relationships*, define boundaries by saying, "In the simplest sense, a boundary is a property line. It denotes the beginning and end of something" (1999, p.17).

Boundaries are solidified limitations or walls that protect you from doing something you don't want to do, saying something you shouldn't say, or being someone you don't desire to be! Boundaries are Amazing and easy to create. However, boundaries are also established to protect you from unwanted people, experiences, and situations that would be detrimental to your life. Boundaries can be applied in every area of your life, including but not limited to your relationships, education, and areas of leadership.

In your relationships, boundaries are important because they protect you and the other person from being hurt or offended. For example, if you're single and ready to mingle but want to be respectful, you could choose not to talk to a single girl or boy after 10 p.m. You create this boundary out of respect for yourself and the other person involved. You would inform the individual that you are interested in conversing with them but during your allocated hours for talking on the phone. As far as your education goes, you could create a boundary of not studying in your bed or doing your homework in class. You choose to set these boundaries because studying in bed is not productive, and doing homework in class may keep you from focusing on what is being taught. As a leader, you can set a boundary between not raising your voice, using foul language, confronting conflict publicly, or treating those you lead with disrespect. Your intent for setting these boundaries is to maintain respect with those you lead, ensure that you lead by example, promoting teamwork and productivity.

The key to maintaining healthy boundaries as a leader is to understand that they aren't permanent. Sometimes you will overstep them or make mistakes. There may be times that you will forget your boundary and talk to that cute girl until midnight. Other times you might choose to study in your bed and fall asleep. You may complete your first block assignment during your fifth block class and completely miss the fact that you have an upcoming quiz. There may even be times when you accidentally raise your voice, say a cuss word, or address a conflict publicly. It's okay; things happen. However, the key to maintaining healthy boundaries is to do your best to keep them. Remember to be flexible and forgive yourself if you overstep them. Keep moving forward, pick up your head, and be the chosen leader you're called to be. As you develop your boundaries, the next component you will need to define is standards.

Standards

Do you live by standards? Have you set up standards that govern your relationships, experiences, lifestyle, and opportunities? If not, it's cool. This is going to help you and increase your self-awareness. Standards are defined as a level of quality or attainment and a rule or principle used as a basis for judgment. This is vital because if you remember this and set up your standards, your life will go to the next level! The great thing about standards is that they can be applied in every area of your life. For example, I expect to graduate with a 4-year degree. Anything less than this is below my standard, which means that I have to work to reach and surpass my standard. Once I do that, I can change my standard. You can make it more practical by applying standards to your classes. You can choose to read for 30 minutes a day, pass courses with nothing less than a B, or turn in all your assignments on time. The goal is to make your standards high enough to make you consistently work and be intentional about maintaining them.

If we continue with the standards we talked about above; you can see how these standards are ones that you set and are holding yourself to. However, not only are you holding yourself to these standards, but you are also consciously and subconsciously holding others to them as well. Imagine if you're chilling at home trying to read a book and somebody calls you. You have two options: you can either stop reading and talk to them or speak to them later. This goes back to having courage. They will respect your standards and gain more respect for you because you are standing up for something you believe in and want to do.

Above we spoke about applying standards to your educational pursuits. You can also apply them to your relationships, whether with friends, families, teachers, bosses, girlfriend/boyfriend, husband, or wife. Standards within relationships are essential because they will help draw the right people into your life and repel the wrong ones. In other words, having standards will attract good people and push bad people away. So, I dare you to take the time to think about your friends. Why are they your friends? What do you all have in common? How did you all meet? Should they still be your friends? I know these are tough questions to answer, and you probably haven't thought about them; however, to be that transformational leader, you have to know the truth.

Michelle Bowman says, "You attract who you are!" Let's run that back for the people in the back, "You attract, who you are!" Before you start canceling friends, relationships, or loved ones, take some time to meditate on that. Take some time to think about what it is about you that connects you to your circle. What is it about you that draws you to them? If your friends are petty, you may be petty yourself! If your friends are angry, you might be a little angry! If your friends are inconsistent, you might be a little inconsistent. However, if your friends are motivated, you're probably motivated! If your friends are excelling in school, you probably are too! If your squad is great, then you're probably great! I DARE YOU TO SHOUT OUTLOUD: I AM GREATTTTTTTTT!!

You are great! You are strong, mighty, capable, fearfully, and wonderfully made! You are amazing, one of a kind, unique, a creator's original, in a class all by yourself. However, nobody will know or even agree if you don't have standards. Remember that standards are the level of quality or attainment and a rule or principle used as a basis for judgment. Therefore, whether in school or personally, your standards indicate your self-worth. If you love yourself, you will have high standards and won't apologize for them! If you love yourself, you will use your standards to guide your friendships, educational pursuits, and personal goals. You won't be ashamed to display them and help others establish their own. Once you've set your boundaries and standards, it's time to establish your non-negotiables.

Non-Negotiables

What I'm about to tell you will change your life forever. Non-negotiables are critical in helping you from settling in life. They are no-nonsense filters for unwanted people, experiences, or opportunities. They are close cousins to boundaries but differ in their intensity and purpose. Non-negotiables are things that are not open for discussion or reconsideration. They are rules or policies that you have put in place to protect or promote a particular way of life.

For example, in relationships, some of your non-negotiables could be that you refuse to date someone younger than you, someone who smokes, or some who is failing in school. In education, some of your non-negotiables could be that you will not attend a college/university further than 6 hours from your hometown. You refuse to take out a student loan. Take electives that you're not interested in, and you refuse to fail a class. Non-negotiables are better established in advance and communicated to those around you so that they can hold you accountable. Again, these non-negotiables are yours, not someone else's. The key is to share them clearly to your friends and family and ensure that they understand your point of view.

Now let me tell you how I am currently applying these principles in my life right now:

I graduated from Columbus Technical College to seek a better path in life. I joined the United States Navy in February of 2010. The military offered me great benefits, a stable job, income, and educational resources so I could pursue it. Year after year, I served well and deployed for months at a time. I've been all over the world to places like Bahrain, Dubai, France, Portugal, Spain, Florida, California, New Jersey, and Virginia, all because of the Navy. It was great! I met some of the most incredible people and have been awarded the opportunity to do one of the world's most fantastic and most dangerous jobs. While enlisted, I advanced reasonably quickly. In less than four years, I went from an E-1 to an E-4 and eventually became an E-6, a First Class Petty officer at my 11-year mark. Life was great, but I wasn't fulfilled. My life was stable, but I wasn't happy! Bills were paid, school was paid for, my car was paid off, purchased a house, but I still wasn't satisfied. I had changed! I was a different Robert than the one that joined in 2010.

See, when I joined the military, I joined to find my life. I didn't know who I was or what I brought to the table. I had no clue about boundaries, standards, or non-negotiables. I was just taking a risk, hoping to find something bigger and better than I had experienced. So as time progressed, I learned, grew, and matured. I experienced highs, lows, victories, and defeats, but they all worked together to make me who I am. I discovered my leadership voice and grew in self-awareness. I learned that I could lead and that people were willing to follow. I realized that I was chosen to be an Author, Speaker, and Pastor. I discovered that I had a passion for entrepreneurship and loved to mentor. Remember, I didn't know these things in the beginning, I learned them along the journey. However, today is Sept 03, 2021, and I am 4 days away from getting out of the military. I am 4 days away from stepping away from structure, stability, and security and into a life of the unknown.

Never settling isn't always about settling for things that are bad or beneath you. Often we settle for things that are good but not great. You know how we settle for a B grade but could've gotten an A. Or how you settle for partially doing your work knowing that you had time to complete it. However, in my case, the Navy was great, but not great enough for what I am Chosen to do.

I am writing to you four days away from a whole new life, and I am excited and nervous. I don't know what I will experience, but I know that it will work out. I chose not to settle for the familiar. It's time for a change. It's time for me to strive for more and seek out the unknown. It's time for me to break away from the comfortable and embrace the uncomfortable. It's my time now, and this is how I want you to think. Now is your time! Never Settle! Just because you did good in something before doesn't mean you can't do better. Just because you made honor roll last semester doesn't mean you can't do it again; keep working. Never stop getting better. YOU ARE YOUR GREATEST INVESTMENT! You deserve the best in life, but you will only get out of life what you put into it. Your boundaries, standards, and non-negotiables support your expectations. You are a Chosen Generation, and you will lead purposefully and change this world for the better! I'll see you in the next chapter!

CHAPTER 7 WORKSHEET

NEVER SETTLE

Having a "never settle" mindset is contagious and will carry you a long way. Defining your boundaries, standards, and non-negotiables will prepare you to be successful in the long run. Therefore, on the lines below, take the time to write down your boundaries, standards, & non-negotiables, and feel free to share them with your friends. You may find that you and your friends share the same things or may differ completely; however, there is no wrong answer. This is your time to display your self-awareness and provide a framework and foundation for your purpose to live.

Boundaries

Boundaries are solidified limitations or walls that protect you from doing something you don't want to do, saying something that you shouldn't say, or being someone you don't desire to be!

1.

_____

_____

_____

2.

_____

_____

_____

3.

_____

_____

_____

Standards

Standards are defined as a level of quality or attainment and a rule or principle that is used as a basis for judgment.

1.

_____

_____

_____

2.

_____

_____

_____

3.

_____

_____

_____

Non-Negotiables

Non-negotiables are things that are not open for discussion or reconsideration. They are rules or policies that you have put in place in your life to protect or promote a particular way of life.

1.

2.

3.

EPILOGUE

You made it! You made it through the journey of Self-awareness, equipping you to be a transformational leader. I hope it was fun and exciting, but I have a secret to tell you. You were already a leader before you read this book. You were already a leader before you flipped a single page. Leadership is natural for you. This book just gave you strategies, principles, and the language to increase your leadership influence by helping you grow in self-awareness. See what you may not know is, is that the most influential leaders are those who are most self-aware. Take people like Steve Jobs, Barack Obama, Lebron James, Serena Williams, Eric Thomas, etc. These people are applauded for what they do, but what they do is not their most incredible gift. Their greatest gift is being self-aware. I know this because I was just like you; young, ambitious, creative, hardheaded, and even stubborn. I knew there was something different about me, but I didn't know what it was. Now I know I was chosen to lead just like you, and I challenge you to lead and walk in your purpose!

This book covered six fundamental principles to help you grow in self-awareness and equip you to be a transformational leader. They were the following:

C- Commit to character

H- Honest about your priorities

O- Open about your emotions

S- Serious about your future

E- Earn to Own

N- Never Settle

If you take these six principles and apply them, I promise you, your life will never be the same. Whether you are a freshman in high school or a graduating college senior, these principles and the information presented will help you make it through the maze of life and equip you to handle the challenges ahead. Remember, you can't do this alone. While you're on this journey to becoming your best self and growing in awareness, bring somebody along the way with you. Find someone around you who needs help and help them. Take somebody up under your wing and teach them these principles. Don't be stingy; share, lol. Seriously, share what you've learned in this book with everyone you know because you never know who needs it.

You're going to be amazed at the results of this transformation. People will begin to treat you differently and comment on your glow! They will begin to say that they see your change and are inspired by you. You will be amazed at the number of opportunities that will come your way and how your relationships will change! Life is about to take a turn for the best! You have to capitalize on this moment and own it! It's for you! You've earned it!

The giant standing before you, in the beginning, is afraid of you now because you have more weapons than you had before. Before, you only had the weapons of your experiences, but now, you have the weapons of awareness! Now, you not only know how to fight, but now you understand why you fight! When things happen in your life now, you will remember the principle of *committing to character*. You won't let someone from your class push you to act out of character. When you face the temptation to do something that will jeopardize your future, you will remember to be *honest about your priorities* and choose not to participate.

If a relationship fails, or you don't get accepted by your desired college, or you fail an exam, you will no longer hold your emotions in and dwell in depression. You've learned how to be *open about your emotions* and have the courage to communicate them to others. As you transition through life, you will no longer just go through without a purpose. You will now be *serious about your future* and be willing to *earn to own*. Your hard work will pay off and drive you to *never settle*. Armed with this mindset, you are unstoppable! Nobody or nothing can stand in your way. YOU ARE A TRANSFORMATIONAL LEADER So don't stop! Take what you learned and excel! I give you the permission to be great! Be a boss! Take Control of your life and be that transformational leader you've been chosen to be! You got this! I believe in you because you are a Chosen Generation!

About the Author

Robert Vann is a country boy from Georgia and the Founder of Discover University, a virtual learning platform dedicated to empowering students to grow in self-awareness, leadership, and purpose. As a Pastor, Mentor, Student, Author, Motivational Speaker, and Veteran, Robert thrives on pursuing his purpose and believes that all should do the same. As a student, Robert earned 3 certificates in Residential Carpentry from Columbus Technical College, 12 Certificates in Non-profit management from Tidewater Community College, and now attends Regent University pursuing a Bachelors in Christian Leadership and Management. He believes that RESILIENCE has gotten him through his successes and hard times and has a mission in life to equip youth and young adults to Discover themselves and inspire all to Change the World in their own way!

For the last 15 years, he has worked with students and young adults to discover their purpose. He also assisted in founding a teen male youth development program named T.C.O. (The Chosen One's.). He currently serves as a Pastor at Ambassadors for Christ Deliverance Center and is an educator for the Norfolk Public School System. He published his first book titled "You are a Strong Man:

Addressing the Pitfalls that Men Face and Providing Tools to Overcome Them" in 2019 and plans on publishing many more.

‣ info@robertbvann.com

‣ www.robertbvann.com

‣ 706-289-6136

‣ Facebook: @AuthorRobertBVann

‣ Instagram: @AuthorRobertBVann

‣ LinkedIn: www.linkedIn.com/in/robertbvann

ACKNOWLEDGMENTS

To the greatest youth I know, I would like to thank Mykell, Josiah, Aniah, Aaliyah, Caliel, all my AFC teens, and all of my students and Blair Middle School for being the inspiration behind this book. You guys are amazing, and I couldn't be who I am without you.

I would like to thank apostle Michelle, the entire ministry staff, and the congregation of ambassadors for Christ deliverance center(AFC) for allowing me to be who I am and supporting me along the way. You guys have taught me that I am special and my voice is needed, and I thank you for always being there.

I would like to thank the Cuffee and Watson family, along with my fellow teachers at Blair and members of AFC for helping me through this publishing process, along with Ms. Bridgett for coaching me through it all. I would like to give a special shoutout to my speaking coach, mike nelson; you are truly amazing and an example/legend in your own way. Thank you for paving the way, and continue to be blessed.

Lastly, I want to thank my parents and family for training me up to be a good man. Without you all, I would not be the man I am, and for that, I honor you!!!

Pick up your copy of the Chosen Generation **_Audiobook_** and **_Video Series_** at www.robertbvann.com/shop

Join our Discover University Family on facebook @DiscoverUniversity!

Robert B. Vann is the Founder of Discover University a virtual education and outreach program that's geared towards equipping students to discover their purpose and grow in self-awareness and leadership skills.

So why did he start Discover University? Well it's simple for him and can be answered by the question, "WHY NOT?" Stemming from a vision given to him by God in 2012 to build a youth and young adult development center, he figured now is as great of a time as ever to start the process of making his dream a reality. With a ton passion, drive, and commitment, Robert understands that starting this University may be crazy to some and understandable for others but he believes that his efforts and those of others are going to leave a legacy for himself, his family, fellow teachers, partners, and the students that are apart of Discover University.